Nov 7th 2020

"If you are born poor its not your fault; if you die poor, its your fault"

-Bill Gates

"When the flow and alignment of your Desire match with the Universe, you become a Law of Attraction In Action, beyond being a positive thinker!"

-Anonymous

"Being relaxed, feeling good and breathing deeply, naturally is one of the most powerful ways to allow joy, well-being, better relationship and yes, more money into your experience"

-Anonymous

ACCELERATE YOUR ABUNDANCE BEYOND "THINK AND GROW RICH"

BECOME A MONEY MAGNET

Babatunde Soluade

Order this book online at www.trafford.com
or email orders@trafford.com

Most Trafford titles are also available at major online book retailers.

Printed in the United States of America.

ISBN: 978-1-4907-4206-9 (sc)
ISBN: 978-1-4907-4205-2 (e)

Trafford rev. 08/27/2014

 www.trafford.com

North America & international
toll-free: 1 888 232 4444 (USA & Canada)
fax: 812 355 4082

Contents

DEDICATION

This book is a light in the tunnel of life for people in the dark or unenlightened, who hardly recognize the power of the mind that could lift them out of financial bondage.

The Universal Law of Infinite Intelligence (God) has made available to every human specie the irreversible inheritance of unlimited resources to make their dreams come true. It now becomes a choice for those who are willing and obedient to tap into those resources.

By global demographic projections, 90% of the world's population appears to be vibrating in the realm of spiritual slumber, making a way for the rich to get richer and the poor to get poorer.

Accelerate Your Victory Beyond Think And Grow Rich is dedicated to reverse this in-balance of power. Power must change hands, and that is why the book is loaded with unprecedented fundamental-mix of doctrines to advance man's strive from poverty to prosperity. It is dedicated to the youths and masses in every society to rise out of spiritual slumber to their full potential, so that this world would be a better place where no man would allow himself to be oppressed.

A wake-up call is a wake-up call, because you can be, do, and have whatever you want in your life. This book is for you to take the first step of faith, even when you do not see the stair-case, and you will be on the way to your promise land. Proceed to read, and follow this book, because your time has come to shine. Enrich!

PREFACE

When I came to Canada in 2011, writing a book was the last thing that ever crossed my mind. I had left behind a thriving security business in Nigeria and it was not possible to replicate a similar type of business in Canada. I decided to change careers and started marketing various wellness products and services. I became a member of many networking groups and as fate would have it, I met a remarkable man in one of such meetings by the name, Gerry Robert. He is the author of the bestseller book "The Millionaire Mindset". His life story is amazing. Coming from a poverty-stricken background, he dropped out of school at age fifteen, to step into the school of life. Ten years down the line, he became an accomplished motivational-speaker and author. Today he is a multi-millionaire in the hundreds, and has shown over three million people how to write a book and grow rich. Gerry suggested I write a book to promote how people can make money and to add as compliment, vital content that recommends a wellness product.

His suggestion hit me like a ton of bricks because I had been voraciously reading many books on those topics. These books were recommended by the Global Information Network (GIN) of Kevin Trudeau in addition to being an independent distributor of Zija International, manufacturers of Moringa Oleifera. Moringa happens to be the most valuable plant in existance. By empirical research results from UNICEF, John Hopkins University and the National Institute of Health (NIH) USA, Moringa can mitigate or reverse over 300 diseases from its rich nutrients. Gerry Robert's suggestions divinely synchronized with my situation because, all of my efforts of the past year prepared me with vital tools for this wonderful opportunity. My first book "Truth and Consequences" was about my life's experience which applied more to a Nigerian/African audience. This second book however has global appeal.

Gerry's suggestion set my adrenalin in motion. For the next ten days, I worked tirelessly and completed my second book. It was at this point that I realized it would be good to achieve success during my lifetime, but even better to leave a legacy.

ACKNOWLEDGEMENT

My first port of call is to recognize the divine authority that directed my steps to meet Gerry Robert, the author of the best-seller book "The Millionaire Mindset", who initiated me into this project in the first place.

Thereafter, assembled along the line, is a plethora of people and places that became instrumental to various modes of contributions, towards the development and completion of the book.

My gratitude goes to my mentor Gerry Robert who sowed the first seed, followed by my family, so suddenly caught unawares by my decision to write a book out of the blues. My admirable wife, Victoria, did not believe it enough to read through to the end under the excuse of book's and I quote, "repetitive characterization" amounting to tautology. Her critique of the book, and to some measure of editing effort, made a massive difference to the re-sequencing of the original script, for which I am most appreciative.

Along the line, my children took their turns to play vital roles at different stages of the work. My brilliant daughter Olufemi schooled me through the technique of doing a video presentation which was new territory. Then Mobolaji my son, who is a creative expert in marketing, guided me on the navigational skills of marketing on the internet, including optimization of contacts transferred to Gmail from my cell phone. Yemisi, my second son, piloted me into opening the first Paypal account, after many futile attempts on my own. All these activities were not familiar territory to me, inspite of my long years of computer experience, where more of the jobs were done by a secretary/staff way back in Nigeria. To these adorable children, I say a big thank you.

In the same vein do I thank my bosom-buddy brother, Professor Oredola Soluade who dutifully edited the introduction part of the book.

By the same token, many thanks go to my friend Rakesh Shrivastava "Rick", a chartered accounting consultant, who's immense interest in my progress, extended the marketing of the book's postings to Craiglist and Kijiji on the internet, to seek partner distributorship in different places.

To the Black Card Publishing Company staff of Gerry Robert, came in so many helping hands. My gratitude goes to Carol Cunliffe, who helped in the search and choice of a domain name that got registered for the website. To Jean-Guy Francoeur, author of "The Messy Manager" and his lovely wife Kerry, whose professional counsel and endorsement I will always cherish and be thankful for. The same sense of gratitude will go to staff members like Matthew and Mary-Beth (author of The

Power of Pets), for their tireless willingness to provide professional counsel at anytime.

To the indefatigable Dr. Godwin Edobor, whose contribution in designing the beautiful website at a virtually low cost, as a gesture of encouraging a viable project, I say a big thank you. Many thanks will apply to the nineteen year-old genius of Korean extraction Sam Seo (CEO of Hostorea Technologies), who re-designed the website with state-of-the-art technology to the next level, of comprehensive interactive global standards.

My very good friend and course-mate at the 3-day Gerry Robert Training, Scott Schlussler voluntarily undertook the task of publishing the book, as well as proof-reading, editing, designing, etc. He filled in many gaps in areas I missed out, during the course. I am most appreciative of his enormous contributions.

A very special thanks will go to David "SuperDave" Ogunnaike. This man is an enigma. The success of this book will be attributed 80% to this man's personal mentorship which was loaded with nuclear wisdom and experience. He succeeded in soft-landing me into the arena of the Millionaire's Club with a gift of his book "The Millionaire Genius", backed by the spiritual fire-power of a $1 million note to set me on fire forever. Thanks a ton SuperDave!

Finally, my thanks go to Gerry Robert especially, the pioneer of this project. He is a phenomenal personality and his wealth of experience and wisdom surpasses money!

Every minute spent with this man is a new school, teaching you what no university in the world can offer. He has changed my life for the better by bringing me to where I want to be, without me being aware ab-initio. Accept my big thank you Gerry.

FOREWORD

When you follow the recipes recommended in this book correctly, then you possess the Winning Attitude to Cause A Realm of New Possibilities to live an Extraordinary life. You are given access to Super-Lucrative Multiple Streams of Income (MSI), for you to pick one and run your business as top priority. For you to succeed, you come to experience improvements in the quality of your personal productivity, wiping out all negative interpretations of contexts (coded as Rackets) to discover a New You. In the process, there is a Positive Permanent Shift in your thinking to empower creativity, in making you unstoppable towards your dreams and desires. It is an opportunity whose time has come to step out of a fixation mind-set, smiling to the bank from unleashing your potential.

Recent research into history has revealed the secret behind long life that became the exclusive privilege of kings and rulers of wealth. Rich nutrients extracted from plants became normal diet for the wealthy, beyond the reach of the masses. Today the story is different. Natural Cures from ancient plants have now been made available through social media platform for anyone to choose which way to go. It is found to be affordable, more pro-active and natural to prolong and rejuvenate lives in ways that can be equated to Miracle Healing. A few will be highlighted at a later stage, including simple regimen that can be practiced under 5 minutes to rejuvenate your body in the comfort of your home. Besides natural cures, these treasures of life can augment exponential increase to your income!

CONCEPT INTRODUCTION AND PURPOSE

Do you want to be rich? Do you want to become a business Titan? Do you want to live a successful lifestyle where money is made to get attracted into your possession? Then you are welcome to a new era of habit-living, as long as you submit to the strange and simple rudiments, sacrosanct for successful wealth-creation, taught in this book. Remember that failure is an orphan and always an unpleasant experience, but success has friends and family to celebrate with, whenever it happens. Success is only a decision away for anyone, who chooses to identify with it. This philosophy applies also, when you want to become a success in making money and so, you must make friends with this book. However, there are certain fundamental parameters that have been established over the ages, which are not known to many or ignored by those who choose to follow their passion, away from the vibrational forces of nature. This book is a new lifestyle, proclaiming peculiar Laws and Ethics that demand compliance, for the speedy acquisition of Wealth. Even in heaven, submission is the first law and there is no reason for anyone to assume that laws of nature in this universe, are not as compelling to inhabitants of our planet here on earth. It is evident that all scriptural texts have Laws. The Bible for example, has ordained the Ten Commandments for Christian worshippers to obey in order to make heaven.

By the same token in the case of money, obedience to the laws that make people rich must be obeyed and practiced correctly. People say that "Practice makes Perfect", but that is not true. What is true is that correct practice makes perfect. In an attempt to practice anything, one must accept the existence of who teaches and who accepts the teaching. In other words, there must be a teacher and a student, or a mentor and an apprentice, just like a master/slave situation. It therefore means that if a student has a bad teacher or an apprentice has the wrong mentor, then the training received will deprive the student of successfully making money, simply because of the wrong tutelage he/she received. That is why a well-articulated formula has been designed and established for any diligent student to follow as a basic training doctrine. This is to ensure anyone can succeed in the practice of wealth creation.

The formula can be summarized as follows:

1. Who you do listen to matters. Listen to people who have what you want.
2. Willingness to learn, and willingness to accept changes of your habits and the way you think.
3. How teachable or coachable can you be? You must be totally willing to follow what you are taught.
4. Training Balance Scale which deals with the Purpose of "WHY" and not "HOW" you want wealth, because the HOW is irrelevant.

5. Master the basic "similar sounding" principles revealed in this book, and become competent in using them.
6. Competence through thorough practice to accomplish your "Mision", in becoming "unconsciously competent".
7. Remain in Robust Health To Enjoy Your Wealth.

You cannot cheat nature in anyway. That is why your journey with this book nurtures your mind to develop new neuro-pathways of thinking habits towards wealth-creation in a very short time. It is a mission that you can only accomplish through disciplined training. This is a training programme that cannot be elaborated enough in great details. The reader has to be willing and obedient to connect with the appropriate consulting experts, or through the Author's Website Training, by visiting www.accelerateyourabundance.com. There is so much information to give, but these Seven Basic Fundamentals are all you need to guide you, and be transformed into a money-magnet.

The therapeutic thrust of Accelerate Your Abundance Beyond "Think and Grow Rich", is to provide the quickest recipe for building a balanced foundation, that enables any serious reader align with the correct principles and precepts of money-making-technology. With such a strong drive, you will easily grow to become wealthy faster than you think. When you finish reading this book, you will not remain the same again. The reason for this is simply because your vibrational frequency would have been involuntarily elevated to a higher gear to dream at the very least, of becoming a money-magnet. You will experience strange positive attractions towards making money, so long as you steadfastly submit to the Highlighted Principles adopted as your Practice Model.

Assume this book as a trusted friend because, it provides and guarantees you the tools, tips, and techniques in navigating a paradigm shift to your ElDorado in the quickest of time.

PURPOSE: The world is inundated with economic crisis generated from un-equal distribution of wealth. In virtually every nation, less than 5% of the people control 90% of the wealth in the community. Apart from violent revolution or systemic evolution which has proved to be a herculean task, bordering on the impossible, all other options has failed. Unknown to many, the Universal Law of Infinite Intelligence (GOD) has opened up the opportunity for the masses to rise to their full potential for self-empowerment to acquire wealth. This can be achieved through pro-active and positive use of their thoughts. That is the only option left for economic power to change hands.

The purpose of this book is a global call set in motion, to change the vibrational frequency of a reader's Mindset into a Positive Behavioral Lifestyle. Such a change will accelerate attraction of wealth into physical existence, so long as the doctrines adopted are diligently complied with. It is a "Mind Mastering Training" of a journey into the Mind of Man.

It is targeted to address people who want to migrate from poverty to prosperity in quick time. People who have surrendered themselves to the belief that lack of financial freedom cannot change hands or that, getting to El Dorado in their lifetime is a "Bridge Too Far", and out of reach. Youths who make up the future of any society essentially need this "Enlightenment Education" through which the spirit of financial freedom and entrepreneurship can be nurtured and better structured.

Many people are anchored in tradition. They find it hard to accept new thinking patterns that could possibly fertilize the "rich garden of their minds", in developing neuro-pathways out of poverty. Having remained stuck to the old school of lack, fear, anxiety for so long, they need a new orientation and education that opens up doors of hope, health, and life of abundance, freely given and freely received. Through transformation of the mind, diligently pursued by purposeful action, anyone can grow rich from obscurity and poverty to the promised land of their dreams.

Now, you can from this point, proceed to join the train of change, in identifying with the summarized precepts of new thinking pathway and habits. This is vitally essential for a successful transformation into becoming a money magnet.

Self-knowers focus to excel at doing what can be equated to the miraculous, because they will always disallow distraction around their lives.

SUPERNATURAL POWER OF FOCUS

Focus is symbolically synonymous with faith through which fear is put to flight. Everybody dreams of El Dorado for financial freedom, health and happiness. El Dorado is a wealthy place which lies at the door of everyman's heart. Your bonanza lies under your feet and all the power you need to achieve your dream comes from within and not from outside of you. Self-knowers always dwell in El Dorado. They drink from the fountains of experience, and are always owners and controllers of their hearts desires because they are no fools. What the fool cannot learn or believe, he laughs at, thinking that by his laughter, he shows superiority instead of latent idiocy. Self-knowers are not like that because of their high level of belief or intense focus, which gives no room for shifting or distraction. The supernatural power of focus can trigger inner forcers into motion to aspire for excellence. It boosts the energy towards your objective which is your "Why", and not in the "How" to get to that objective. Such excellence becomes a remarkable feat, which can be equated to the miraculous!

What you focus on expands what you ignore diminishes.

Power-house of conviction and energy to build belief and conviction for creation is the subconscious mind. You were created to add value to creation.

THE SUBCONSCIOUS MIND

The subconscious mind is a power-house in the chemistry of believing. The conscious mind works in the brain when you are thinking while the subconscious works while you are sleeping, or relaxing on other tasks. The decision of the" subconscious mind" is faultless due to its inherent elements of instinct, reflex and accumulated experience. The way the conscious mind is the source of thought, so is the subconscious the source of power. The subconscious is a powerhouse of energy through which an individual can recover his strength, courage and faith in himself. The subconscious combines the feeling of wisdom of the past, the awareness and knowledge of the present, and the thought and vision of the future. The judgment of the "subconscious mind" which represents inherent instincts and the accumulation of experience is virtually infallible in comparison with conscious thinking. The possibilities of creative effort connected with the subconscious mind are stupendous and imponderable. If you fail to plant favorable desires in your subconscious mind, it will feed upon the thoughts that reach it as a result of neglect.

You are persuaded to form the habit of applying and using positive emotions (thoughts). With time, the positive will dominate your mind so completely to block the negative from entering.

Good gesture begets good return. Connect with people who have what you want. Be teachable.

LAW OF RECIPROCITY

In human relationship, think and believe that the other fellow is a fine person and that is what he will turn out to be. Do not reject this great truth. Just apply it and you will be amazed at the startling results. The basic law of reciprocity remains constant in life's experience. You can experiment with a dog by patting him with kindness . . . The dog will wag his tail in appreciation, and he will try to lick your hand or face if you give him a chance. The reaction of people is similar, when you give sincere compliments. You will be bound to receive friendly gesture in return. Cultivate a new character to be a carrier of good news and good gesture.

This same truth applies to wealth creation. A person who desires riches must go to where riches are. If you want money, you have to associate yourself with people who have it or who know how to make it. Make an effort to become personally acquainted with those who have wealth or who control the authority to spend money. Use the opportunity to submit and work in total obedience to be teachable by your mentors. Lift your "Teachability Index" to the limits and always endeavor to recognize wherever you are, as a stepping stone to a great future.

Positively vaccinate yourself against failure on the grounds of health, intelligence, age or luck.

ANTIDOTE TO EXCUSE DISEASE

Vaccinate yourself against the disease of failure, called "Excusitis". It starts with worrying about some kind of problem which leads to lack of confidence. Every minute a person spends worrying about failure is a period of waste. Worry leads to killing a "success" potential to accept defeat. Worry is a bad attitude. There is an adage that says, "The right attitude with one arm will beat the wrong attitude with two arms all the time", which has become a fact of life. Excusitis appears in a variety of forms but the worst types are in the areas of health, intelligence, age, and luck. But worry can be overcome. The Antidote that applies to the most significant of all is the Health aspect, whose experts have postulated the following "advice" statements:

1. Refuse to talk about any ill health in your body.
2. Refuse to worry about your health.
3. Be genuinely grateful for a good health.
4. Remind yourself that life is yours to enjoy and you will not waste it with worry.

The second category is in the area of "Intelligence Excusitis". This is where people sell themselves short by under-estimating their own and other fellow's brain power. The thinking that guides your intelligence is more important than the quality of your brain or how much intelligence you may have. The ability to know how to get intelligence is more important than using the mind as a garage of facts; just like an idea man can make money where a fact man cannot do the same. The cure to intelligence excusitis can be summarized as follows:

1. Discover your superior talents as your asset and focus on it. Manage your brain instead of worrying about how much IQ you have.
2. Your attitude is more important than your intelligence. Develop the "I am winning attitude", and put your intelligence to creative positive use.
3. Ask yourself this question "Am I using my mental ability to make history or am I using it merely to record history made by others?

In the case of "Age Excusitis", how old we are is not important. It is one's attitude towards age that makes it a blessing or a barricade. When you beat down the fear of age limitation, you add years to your life as well as success. If you practice looking forward to new horizons, you will gain enthusiasm and the feeling of youth particularly, if you must invest your time in doing what you really want to do.

There is also the case of "Luck Excusitis" which has become a norm in people's lives, without giving thought to the law of cause and effect. Nothing happens without a cause and it has to be understood in its proper perspective. Good luck is preparation, planning, and success-producing thinking, to precede good fortune.

This is what people identify as good luck. This is what makes the difference between Mr. Success and Mr. Failure. Mr. Success receives a setback, learns from it and profits. Mr. Failure (mediocre) loses but fails to learn! Success comes from doing things and mastering them as principles adopted for success, or as lessons learnt, never allowed to re-occur.

Mirror Technique to repeatedly remind and rehearse positive thoughts, actions and pronouncements. You will be able to do all presentations without trepidation.

DISCOVER A NEW YOU

Paste slips of paper with positive slogans on your mirror where everyone can see when entering your room or office. Slogans such as "Nothing is impossible to an indefatigable mind", "I am going to Win", "I will show the world I am not licked". Next step is to stand before a mirror of full length or half length; like a soldier coming to salute on a parade ground. Breathe in deeply, three or four times, until you feel a sense of power, strength and determination. Look into the very depth of your eye to tell yourself what you want aloud, so you can see your lips move and hear the words. Make it a regular ritual as many times a day, and you will be surprised at the results. This can be augmented by using soap to write on the mirror of your bathroom, what keywords you wish to express. Within a few days, you will have developed a sense of confidence that you never realized you could build. Use this same technique when making presentation or going for an interview, until you are convinced you can make a proper presentation without trepidation. If you are to make a speech, you must practice before a mirror. Gesticulate; pound your fist on the palm of your hand to drive home the argument, and use any other gesture that comes naturally to you. As you stand before the mirror, keep telling yourself that you are going to be an outstanding success. This practice quickens your subconscious to get the idea and sooner, your wish becomes a picture of power. Develop eyes that bespeak confidence using the mirror to help you. If you have poor posture or are incoherent in your talk, you will find practice before a full-length mirror will work wonders for you. In some nights just before dropping to sleep, order the subconscious mind to bring you an answer. You may awaken up in the middle of the night or in the morning, or another time with the answer. Be quick to grasp it when it comes, then waste no time in following through with it.

Take positive action decisively and promptly. Consistently count your blessings before you sleep at night.

OVERCOMING FEAR

Fear is success enemy number one. It wears down physical vitality, makes people sick, shortens life, closes your mouth when you want to speak, and increases worry and tension. But fear can be defeated. When you see people who radiate confidence and have conquered worry, it was acquired by actively training their minds over time. Action cures fear while indecision and postponement fertilize fear. All you need do is to isolate fear and take appropriate action. Take action promptly and decisively because hesitation magnifies the fear. The best approach against fear dilemma is a two-way traffic of deposit and withdrawal. But you must deposit only positive thoughts in your memory bank. Successful people specialize in putting positive thoughts into their memory bank because, negative thoughts produce needless wear and tear on their mental motor. Negative thoughts put you beside the road while others pass you by. Count your blessings before you sleep and joy will come in the morning. You don't need mental monsters in your memory bank to break down your confidence.

It is important to develop an understanding attitude by getting a balanced view of people and places. People have more similarities than differences. This approach can be adopted as a habit of doing the right thing all the time, complimenting a fundamental factor for success.

Change your thinking from the "Imprisoning Mindset" to the "Action Model" by the following suggested confessions:

1. I can't changes to I Will.
2. Resentment changes to Gratitude.
3. Desire for sympathy changes to Desire for Accomplishment.
4. Dwelling on "It's Not Fair" changes to Search for Opportunities.
5. Acceptance changes to Invention.
6. "Maybe tomorrow . . . ," changes to Do It Now.
7. Withdrawal changes to Participation.
8. Depression changes to Celebrations of Even Small Victories.

Taking a front seat at meetings is considered a confidence-building vitamin. The same applies with making eye contact during discussions or walking faster by twenty-five percent, speaking up during discussions, and putting energy to your smile to come alive!

Read aloud repeatedly, written positive affirmations in changing your mental picture to feed the "rich garden of your subconscious mind".

AUTOSUGGESTION

The principle of autosuggestion is another approach of applying imagination to translate your desire into physical reality. Repetitive words and phrases read silently or aloud are merely methods of convincing the subconscious mind. The simpler the words the better. Examples are like saying to yourself, "I am happy"; "I am strong", repeatedly twenty to thirty times. These few positive affirmations can be used to change your mental picture for the better and may continue until the desired results are obtained. Just pursue the thoughts unceasingly to drive the suggestion deeply and firmly into the subconscious mind, which accepts whatever it is powerfully instructed to do. You must at all times fill your mind with positive thoughts. That way, strong vibrations will ward off all negative and destructive thoughts that might come from outside. It is necessary to close the door of yesterday and keep it closed. We live today and not yesterday.

Autosuggestion is simply gathering of positive thoughts stated in writing. It is the agency of control through which an individual may voluntarily feed the subconscious mind, thoughts of creative nature or by neglect, thoughts of destructive nature to find their way into the" rich garden of the mind". When you read aloud the written statement of your desire for money to see and feel you are in possession of it, then you are communicating your desire to the subconscious, in the spirit of faith. Through repetition of this procedure, you voluntarily create thought habits favorable to your effort, to transmute desire to monetary equivalent. In order to succeed with autosuggestion are these instructional hints that must be followed in the spirit of faith or strong belief:

1. Go to a quiet spot preferably in bed at night to read aloud repeatedly the amount you intend to accumulate. As you carry out these instructions, see yourself already in possession of the money.

2. Repeat the rehearsal night and morning until you see the money you intend to accumulate

3. Place a written copy of your statement where you can see it most of the time. Read it just before retiring and upon rising until it has been memorized. When you follow these rules the way you are told, your skepticism will soon be replaced by belief and this in turn will crystallize into absolute faith. Then you will have arrived at the point where you may truly say "I am the Master of my Fate, I am the Captain of my soul". Carry out these instructions as though you were a small child with the faith of a child.

Paste inspiring pictures and cards around your bed-side or wallet in your office and room as a constant reminder of your fulfilled desires.

PAINT A PICTURE

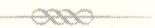

It is reported that F. W. Woolworth recognized as the "Napoleon" of the business world made his office a replica of Napoleon's study. This goes to serve as a constant inspiring reminder that Woolworth can succeed as "Napoleon" did succeed. There is a motto or slogan to meet his gaze every time he looks around the room, as well as a touch of the spiritual, to excite his imagination through the subconscious mind. In many clinics, doctors are known to hang photographs of great men of medicine or renowned experts of the medical profession.

Coming down to the mechanics, it is good to try this example. Secure three or four business-size cards and on each, write one thing you desire above everything in your life with a word picture at the top. Carry one in your hand bag/wallet and another alongside your bed. Place another on your shaving mirror and at your desk. This will enable you mentally see the picture at all hours of the day to visualize your desire into speedy materialization. At the start, you may have no idea of how the results are to come. Just leave it to the subconscious mind which has its own way of making contacts, and of opening doors and avenues that you may never contemplate. You will receive assistance from the most unexpected sources. You may get the idea of writing a letter or making a telephone call. Whatsoever the idea, it is good to follow it up whether it came during the night or day.

Ask and you shall receive. Allow your Well Being to flow in Harmony with Universal Laws of Vibration, making your desire and belief a vibrational Match. Your request or desire is answered every time you ask without question. Your Well Being is naturally your Legacy and your Source.

LAW OF ATTRACTION

Your emotions provide a wonderful guidance system for you. If you pay attention to these emotions, you will be able to guide yourself to anything that you desire. Paying attention to the way you feel, you can easily know if you are giving attention to your desire or if you are giving it to the absence of that desire. Success is what you attract by the person you become. If you are predominantly thinking about the things that you desire, your life experience reflects those things. The Law of Attraction is synonymous with the Law of Reflection. Nothing can occur in your life experience without your invitation of it through your thoughts. You must begin to accept yourself as a Vibrational Being, because this is a Vibrational Universe. Once you become consciously at one with the Universal Laws, all mystery and confusion will be replaced by clarity and understanding. Doubt/fear will be replaced by knowledge and confidence; uncertainty will be replaced by certainty, and joy will return as your premise of experience. Your desires and belief must be a vibrational match for you to receive what you desire.

The Bible says, "Ask, and you shall receive". In this case, as the scripture says, "your request or desire is heard and answered every time without exception". Without asking, you will receive no answer. It is necessary for you to discover your innate ability to allow the Well-Being of this Universe to flow seamlessly into your awareness, which is sometimes called the Art of Allowing. Open the floodgates of your mind and let your Well Being flow in. This Art is the technique of no longer limiting the Well-Being that you deserve, which naturally is your Legacy, your Source, and your very Being. There is unlimited stream of Well Being and abundance of good offers available to you all the time. To receive them depends absolutely on your desire to receive them. Your mind must be in alignment of receiving them all the time.

Imagine and plan with confidence a burning desire to get rich. Develop wealth awareness because there is money everywhere.

COMMAND YOUR WISH

The starting point of all achievements and first step to riches is desire. Desire for riches can be transmuted into financial equivalent through the following practical steps:

1. Don't wish it were easier, wish you were better.
2. Determine an amount you want and what you want to give in return.
3. Establish a definite date when you intend to possess the money.
4. Don't wish for less problems, wish for more skills to navigate to the desired goal of your plans.
5. Don't wish for less challenges, wish for more wisdom to follow your plans.
6. Visualize and command the money into existence with absolute confidence.
7. By imagination, celebrate with gratitude as if you have, and it will come in due time.

Accumulation of money cannot be left to chance, good fortune or luck. There must be definiteness of purpose, knowledge of what you want, and a burning desire to possess it before money will appear. If you do not see great riches in your imagination, you will never see them in your bank account. You must always kindle in your mind the fire of hope, faith, courage and tolerance, because you are an excellent person who deserves success. Imagine yourself successful by visualizing the person you want to become. Set aside each day to be alone and undisturbed to close your eyes and concentrate on your desires and goals. Follow this up by celebrating your past success which you recall when you begin to lose faith. Have a clear direction where you want to go and then take immediate action. Develop a positive self image in all circumstances, backed by enduring faith in your success and your desire for money will manifest itself!

Choose thoughts that make you feel good when you think them. Control how you can feel good in the midst of your experience to progress towards Creation of your happiness.

HUNTER OF HAPPINESS

In an attempt to reach for bliss, you must surely align with the Energy of your source and in that constant alignment, your Well-Being is assured. You have the ability to direct your thoughts to imagine things as you want and distract from what you don't want. You must always pay attention and deliberately choose thoughts about everything that makes you feel good when you think them. When you feel good, good fortune follows you. You have the ability to direct your own thoughts, with the option to imagine them the way you want them to be. It is possible to distract yourself from something you don't want and put your attention on something wanted. Once you understand these Laws of Cosmic Vibration, and how to control how you can feel good by choice in the midst of your experience, then you are making progress towards creation to achieve your desires. You must encourage yourself to become a hunter of Happiness.

Stimulate your imagination by visualizing pleasant situations to delight your mind. Use virtual reality to activate new vibrations.

REMOTE REALITY

This is synonymous with visualizing or conjuring, but with the singular intention of pleasing yourself as you do so. As you practice this process and stimulate your imagination more, you will find it a delightful good-feeling way to spend time. You can make your vibration change for the better on a number of subjects, to reflect wonderful improvements. Remote Reality which is sometimes called Virtual Reality is the practice of visualizing pleasant scenes in your mind to make those good-feeling vibrations become your target practice. Since the universe responds to your vibrations, amazing things can begin to flow into your experience in an unprecedented way. There is nothing more important than that you feel good; and there is nothing better than creating images that can cause you to feel good. The purpose is to cause you to activate new vibrations within you that you put in a place of allowing your Well-Being. Do not use this process to improve a specific existing situation, because in your attempt to fix something, you will bring your existing vibration into your new Virtual Reality, which could be conflicting in all likelihood . . . Once you have practiced Virtual Reality, it will be easy for you to reach for a specific thought that makes you feel better.

Rise above trivialities. Stimulate your mind by reading books regularly. See beyond how things appear at the moment.

DEPTH OF VISION

Confidence in yourself to make you think great within the wider picture can be attributed to the following:

1. Never ever sell yourself short.
2. Use positive, cheerful words and phrases to describe how you feel. Words that promise victory, hope, happiness and pleasure.
3. Use bright, cheerful, favorable words and phrases to describe other people.
4. Use positive language to encourage people by complimenting them personally at every opportunity.
5. See what can be and not what it is. Get the bigger picture. Stretch your vision by adding value to things, people and places.
6. Think above trivial things. Before getting involved in a petty matter, ask yourself, "Is this really important?"
7. You must cultivate the habit of reading for the simple reason that the more you read, the greater your thinking faculty is stimulated.

By practice of Positive Vision Objectives, the Law of Attraction will start drawing great things into your life.

Act; think that you are important and wealthy. Build a "sell yourself to yourself commercial" to be reminded you are a first-class person.

UPGRADE YOUR PROFILE

There are so many ways of upgrading your profile. First is to look important because your appearance speaks about you. Be sure your appearance lifts your spirits and builds your confidence. Always make sure your appearance talks to others with the impression that you are prosperous and dependable. Secondly, think that your work is strategically important and your subordinates and associates will think the same way. The third part is to give yourself a pep talk several times a day in front of a mirror. Build a "sell yourself to yourself" commercial to be reminded that you are a first-class person. Fourthly ask yourself in every situation this question, "Is this the way an important and wealthy person thinks?" Thereafter, obey whatever is the answer you get.

Have a mind of your own, but make quick decisions. Develop a listening habit and keep your mouth shut when you need to learn.

RESOLUTIONS

Procrastination, the opposite of decision is a common enemy that practically everybody must conquer and avoid. To be successful in business, you must cultivate the habit of reaching decisions promptly and changing those decisions slowly if and when they are changed. People, who fail to accumulate money without exception, have the habit of reaching decisions very slowly if at all they try. Such people change those decisions quickly and often. Have a mind of your own to reach decisions. If you need facts or information from other sources as you probably will from time to time, acquire these facts quietly without disclosing your purpose. Keep your eyes wide open and your mouth closed if you wish to acquire the habit of prompt decision. If you talk more than you listen, you not only deprive yourself of many opportunities to accumulate knowledge, but you disclose your plans and purposes to people who will take delight in defeating your plans and strategy. Genuine wisdom is usually conspicuous through modesty and silence. It is wise to first show the world what you want to do before you say it.

Become a Dream Builder by appealing to your imagination. Give life and action to new ideas and you are building a dream.

DREAM BUILDING

God seems to throw himself on the side of people who know exactly what they want if they are determined to get just that idea. Idea is an impulse of thought that impels action by an appeal to the imagination. Ideas can be sold where merchandise cannot. For example, a publisher changed the name of one book that was not moving in the market, and his sales jumped upwards of more than a million copies. He merely ripped the cover bearing the title that did not sell, and put on a new cover with a new title that had box-office value. Just an idea by imagination because idea is a product of imagination! Ideas can be transmuted into cash through the power of definite purpose plus definite plans. All that is required is to give life, action and guidance to ideas, and it will take on power of its own, sweeping aside all oppositions. Begin to nurture the idea and habit of a Dream Builder to attract signs and wonders into your life, and you are on the road to becoming a money-magnet!

Always think positively to radiate happiness. Anyone you are holding as your object of attention inherits your vibration.

GREATEST GIFT

Your happiness is the greatest gift you can ever give to anyone. When you are connected to the stream of pure positive source of Energy that is truly you, then your joy comes full-cycle and complete. In such a state of connection, anyone that you are holding as your object of attention benefits from your attention. Your happiness does not depend on what others do but on your vibrational balance, between your desires, and your vibrational offering which you have launched. Only when you pay attention to the way you feel, can you guide yourself steadily toward your own goals. When you give attention to something that you desire, and you say yes to it, you are including it into your vibration by Law of Attraction.

Be an activationist. The few who do, are the envy of the many who watch.

ACTION HABIT

Be an activationist. A fair idea acted upon and developed is 100% better than a terrific idea that dies because it is not followed up. Use action to kill fear. Gain confidence to see fear disappear. People who get things done in this world don't wait for the spirit to move them; they move the spirit by taking action to "dig in". An excellent way to move the spirit when you want to think is by writing. Seize this initiative to become a crusader. Do what you fear and fear disappears. Always deal and think in terms of now. Tomorrow, next week, later are words synonymous with the failure word "never", and so be the "I am starting right now" kind of person. Better still, you could put these few Wisdom Statements to use for inspiring your spirit into action:

1. Speak Action into existence daily to bring and build belief.
2. Action is your Fuel to success.
3. Action creates habit, and habit creates Character.
4. Your business will not move if you do not put your game plan into Action.
5. An ounce of action is worth a ton of theory.
6. Action will delineate and define you.
7. Positive Action and Passion for Money makes you a Money Magnet.

A Prosperity Game (PGP) and powerful tool to fire and expand your desire and vibrational point of attraction towards wealth.

THE NUMBER'S GAME

This is called the Prosperity Game Process (PGP), operated by establishing an imaginary checking account to make deposit entries and check withdrawals as if it were an actual account. Prepare imaginary checkbooks and deposit slips. On the first day, deposit $1,000 and spend it to buy whatever appeals to you. It could be in one check or several, depending on your choice. The essence of this game is to have fun thinking about what you want to buy. Keep a record book on all these transactions and be descriptive on the memo portion of the check to show the items purchased. You are encouraged to spend as you like because every other day, you will make deposits according to the exact number of that day in the queue, since you started. It will lead to days, weeks and months as this example demonstrates:

1. On second day you deposit $2,000.
2. On third day you deposit $3,000.
3. On fourth day you deposit $4,000.
4. On 50th day you deposit $50,000.

If you play this game for one year, you will have deposited more than $66 million! As you play this game for a few weeks, your ability to imagine will expand tremendously. In playing this game you will find yourself reaching for more new ideas and in time, you will feel the expansion of your own desires and expectations, thus shifting your point of attraction. It is a Prosperity Game Process and a powerful tool for shifting your vibrational point of attraction. Your life experience will shift. You can play this game anyway you want because there are no strict rules. Spend as much as you would want but, ensure you exercise your imagination the best way you can. At the end of the day, the game will cause you to offer more expansive vibration-creating manifestations of wealth, in response to your changed vibration, raising your level of imagination to attract money!

Power is derived from a group of collected brains working in harmony.

STRONGHOLD OF THE MASTERMIND

Power is essential for success in the accumulation of money. Power may be defined as organized and intelligently directed knowledge, sufficient to enable an individual to translate desire into its monetary equivalent. Organized effort is produced through the coordination of two or more people who work in harmony towards a common goal. Master Mind principle holds the secret of the power wielded by people who surround themselves with other people of brains. The psychic part of Master Mind culminates when a group of individual brains is coordinated and functions in harmony. The culmination happens when the increased energy created through that alliance becomes available to every individual brain in the group. It can be likened to spiritual anointing to every member of a worship congregation. A typical example is Henry Ford who whipped poverty, illiteracy and ignorance by allying himself with great minds, whose vibration of thought he absorbed into his own mind. Through association with Thomas Edison, Firestone, Burbank, Mr. Ford added to his own brain power the sum and substance of the intelligence, experience, knowledge and spiritual forces of these men. The same can be said of Mahatma Ghandi who accomplished a historic feat by the induction of

200 million people to cooperate in a spirit of harmony and work towards a definite objective. They placed themselves in a position through an alliance, to absorb power and belief directly from the great universal storehouse of Infinite Intelligence. By this process, they acquired motivation in harmony, and India became free of British rule.

Killing Time is not "murder", it is "suicide". Time is more than money and so you must programme and have purpose for every available moment.

TIME

People often complain about lack of time when lack of direction is the real problem. Many "experts" claim we should be arrested for murder when we kill time. Close examination, however makes it obvious that killing time is not murder; it is Suicide. Time can be an ally or an enemy when you come to terms with accepting that your time is your life, and your life is your time. Time is precious and must be respected more than money. That is why the Bible breaks it into seasons for a reason—there is time to cry, there is time to die, and there is time to celebrate and so on. Time is the spirit behind the concept of Punctuality so that activities can be synchronized and harmonized into a set pattern or purposed-based programmes. What time becomes depends entirely upon you, your goals and your determination to utilize every available minute.

Remove the word "impossible" from your dictionary and cancel out "traditional thinking" from your mindset. Practice listening more than talking to obtain raw materials for creativity.

CREATIVITY

It is simply finding new improved ways to do something. When you think something can be done, it sets the mind in motion to find a way to do it, thereby paving the way for creative solution. Where there is a will, there is a way. In the process of creative thinking, the word "impossible" must be avoided because it sets a chain reaction of other thoughts to disprove you are right. It is therefore necessary to become receptive to new ideas and to abort traditional thinking. You must be able to break routine and become an experimental person, looking out for new things. Build capacity by proving to yourself that how much you can do depends on how much you think you can do. Practice asking and listening. You have two ears and one mouth, so you must use them proportionally. By listening, you will obtain raw materials for sound decisions. Big people monopolize the listening while small people monopolize the talking. Stretch your mind by mixing with people of different occupational and social interest. Your creativity develops from a deliberate departure from old habits and thought patterns. If you think and do the same things of the past all the time, it means you are stagnating and not growing. Creativity is the engine room for making money just like in other aspects of life, when you subject new ideas to practical tests.

Be fearful and RETREAT, or Be empowered and ACT.

BELIEF LEVEL

Faith builds up belief level and has many definitions. Basically Faith starts with confidence in the absence of evidence. Other interesting definitions are expressed as follows:

1. Faith is the basis of all "miracles" and mysteries that cannot be explained by the rules of science.
2. Faith is the only known antidote to fear. Faith and Fear are strange bed-fellows.
3. Faith is the element or chemical which when mixed with prayer give direct communication with Infinite Intelligence.
4. Faith is the only agency through which cosmic force of Infinite Intelligence can be harnessed and used.
5. Faith is taking the first step even when you don't see the staircase.

Every one of the foregoing statements is capable of proof. It is also known fact that one comes to finally believe what one repeats to oneself, be it true or not. Each of us is what we are because of the dominating thoughts we permit to occupy our minds. A thought thus "magnetized" with emotions may be compared with a seed that is planted on fertile ground, germinates and grows to multiply. From the great storehouse of the ether, the human mind is constantly attracting vibrations that harmonize that which dominates the mind. When you take an inventory of your mental assets and liabilities, you will discover that your greatest weakness is lack of self-confidence, derived from dominant negative thoughts of past experiences. This timidity can be surmounted and translated into courage through the principle of Autosuggestion discussed earlier. Begin to replace these negative thoughts with the positive ceaselessly until the positive becomes the dominant thoughts. At this stage, your new belief level (Faith) will empower you to move mountains with confidence. You must remember that confidence practiced over time builds competence. The practice of competence gets you to the level of "Unconscious Competence". You will command money into your life and it will be answered in due time.

Appreciating pleasant objects and happenings around you in gratitude gives you good feelings, accumulating to Rampage Of Appreciation. It is the fastest way to connect with the source of Non-Physical Energy.

RAMPAGE OF APPRECIATION

Life is not about tomorrow, it is about right now that you are currently creating Energy. Try to hold your attention on pleasant objects around you and consider how beautiful, wonderful or useful they look. As you focus upon the object longer, your positive feelings increase. Deserving to have an improved condition is essential, but appreciating what is already good in your life brings more of what is good to you. No matter what happens, you can always find a small thing to appreciate and you can build from there. The more you practice appreciation, the less resistance you will have in your vibrational frequencies. You must always mix Appreciation with Gratitude because by the practice of Appreciation, you will become accustomed to the feelings of higher vibrations. It would be a good idea to set aside a few minutes during the day to practice this just because it feels good and pleasing. As you continue to appreciate, you will find something else to appreciate until in time, you are experiencing Rampage of Appreciation. The more you find something to appreciate, the better it feels. Practicing this process with Gratitude would cause you to practice the Art of Allowing unconsciously, and all good things about your desire will begin to manifest into your experience. This means you have actually set your vibrational frequency to a level of allowing what you asked for into your experience and the Source has answered. You are now in the last step of "letting in" or "Creation". It is the easiest and fastest way to connect the source of Non-Physical Energy and at this point, you are hands-on creator that you have come to be. Your blessings begin to multiply turning your desires to monetary equivalent of your wishes to create wealth.

*There is no lacking but abundance with the universe.
Develop abundance consciousness all the time*

UNLIMITED RESOURCES

This is what the Universe always offers and it is a Constant. The Universe is full of Abundance of everything that is needed. There is no shortage of resources neither is there competition for resources. It is a matter of alignment. Once a person having a desire is in alignment with his own request, that person will experience no shortage or lack. By imaging the existence of that desire with intense focus and belief, the Universe will create circumstances and situations (resources) towards the realization of his desire. There is only the allowing or disallowing of that which you are asking for.

A group of special people working in harmony for a common purpose, make everyone in that group knowledgeable and special. Formal education makes you a living but self-education makes you a fortune.

COLLABORATIVE KNOWLEDGE

Knowledge will not attract money unless it is organized and intelligently directed through practical action plans towards the definite end of wealth accumulation. Lack of understanding of this fact has been the source of confusion to many people who falsely believe that knowledge is power. Any person is educated who knows where to get knowledge when needed and how to organize that knowledge into plans of action. Formal education can get you a living, but self-education can get you a fortune! Henry Ford through the assistance of his "Master Mind" had at his command all the specialized knowledge he needed to enable him become one of the wealthiest men in America. The person who can organize and direct a "Master Mind" group of people who possess knowledge, useful in the accumulation of money, is just as much an educated person as anyone in the group. Remember this if you suffer from inferiority complex about limited schooling. Thomas Edison the inventor of incandescent light and one of the greatest inventors ever, had only three months of schooling in his life, while Henry Ford from very poor background had very limited education.

Powerful tool for boosting your feelings of prosperity and financial point of attraction.

THE WALLET TECHNIQUE

This is a technology to apply when you want to attract more money into your life's experience. Wallet Process will help you offer a vibration that is compatible with receiving money rather than pushing it away. First obtain a $100 bill and put it in your wallet. Keep it there at all times. By holding the $100 bill and not spending it right away, you receive a vibrational advantage of it every time you think of it. In ignoring the urge to purchase anything, you have mentally spent $100 bill 20 or 30 times enabling you to receive the vibrational advantage of having spent $3,000. Each time you acknowledge that you have the power right there in your wallet to purchase again and again, you add to your sense of financial well being and so your point of attraction begins to shift. You do not have to actually be abundant in order to have abundance. By mentally spending the money again and again, you practice the vibration of well being, of security, of abundance, of financial security and the universe responds to the vibration you have achieved. Seemingly magical things will begin to happen as soon as you achieve that wonderful feeling of financial abundance. In time you will experience as if a floodgate of abundance has opened, wondering where all that was hiding.

This is the simple but powerful process and it will change your financial point of attraction. Although there is no limit to what the Universe will yield, you have to feel good about great abundance before you will allow the pleasure of great abundance to flow into your experience. While you move through your day wondering how many things you could spend $100 bill on, you are deliberately utilizing the Non-Physical Energy to enhance your feeling of prosperity. You spend $100 one thousand times a day and you have spent the equivalent of $100,000, which will bolster your feeling of prosperity.

Develop love when paying your bills. Let the spirit of Love guide your attitude towards money in all circumstances.

FEEL AFFECTION TOWARDS MONEY

The better you feel towards money, the more money you magnetize to yourself. Adopt a positive attitude towards your bills. When you pay your bills, find a way, anyway to feel good. Never pay your bills feeling bad because you will be bringing bigger bills to yourself. You need to use your imagination to turn your bills into something that makes you feel better. You can imagine that they are not bills at all, but you have decided to donate money to people out of the goodness of your heart, because of the wonderful service they provided. Use gratitude and give thanks to the company who sent you the bill, by thinking about a good service received.

When some money comes into your hands, be grateful for it no matter how small. Remember whatever you are grateful for multiplies. Gratitude is a good multiplier. Seize every moment that you are handling money to make the money multiply by feeling good. Feel love when you pay for anything.

Imagine the front of a dollar bill as the positive side which represents plenty of money, while the back represents lack of money. When you handle the money, make sure the front is facing upward. By doing so you are using money as your cue to remember to feel good about plenty of money. If you are using credit card, then flip the credit card to the front where your name is, because the front of your card is telling you that there is abundance of money and it has your name on it.

Imagine that you are wealthy right now. Imagine that you have all the money that you need right now. How would you live life differently? Think about the things you would do. You would feel different and because you would feel different, you would walk, talk, think, move and react different to everything. That is the feeling of love for money.

Remember whenever another person receives more money or succeeds, get excited and celebrate with him because it means you are on the same frequency. If you rejoice for the other person, you are saying yes to more money and success to yourself.

If you give away money without expecting returns and you give it with a feeling of love when you give it, most surely it will return to you in multiple measure. It is not how much you give that matters, it is how much love you put into the giving. You must be a prominent partaker in connecting with your community by way of cheerfully and generously donating to its Charity Development Programmes and beyond because, it will always return with good measure in multiple folds.

AFFIRMATIONS

This is the Ultimate Practice. Write a statement of the amount of money of your Dreams at least, 30 times every morning without fail. If you can extend it to two or three times a day, the bigger the benefits that will accrue in the vibration of your mind. Mix this exercise with "Appropriate Actions" consistently. Within a period of three months of consistent practice, you will begin to experience peculiar promotional developments transmuting your efforts towards favorable financial increase!

Alternatively, you can use "Thunder Affirmations" after the Quick Summary at the end of this book to confess aloud at least Ten Times (10) a day with the power of conviction. When you back such powerful pronouncements with appropriate action, you get the same results.

ROAD MAP

UNLIMITED SUCCESS ACCESS

Now that you are conversant with the rudiments inherent in the build-up to become a money magnet, it is time to take a leap into applying those dynamic laws practiced by millionaires and billionaires of history, across the world. Assume at this point in time, that you have now adopted a Road Map, towards achieving UNLIMITED SUCCESS, in the pursuit of wealth creation.

These laws are tested, studied and followed by the wealthy and successful, which will be shared with you. If we are not where we want to be financially, then what we are doing and the result we are getting, need to change.

Albert Einstein confirmed this in a statement quote, "The definition of insanity is doing the same thing over and over and expect different results", unquote . . . So if we can start a project with the right mindset, then we are setting ourselves up for success right from the outset. People who feel that emphasis about attitude in any endeavour is a waste of time always miss the mark. They only want emphasis on 'how to' or 'specifics' on a business topic, and almost always end up as failures.

Experts of Harvard Business School (HBS) claim that psychology and attitude are paramount to your success and probably, more important than all the "tips" and "secretes" you are looking for. Once you have the right mindset, you will always find the 'how to'.

Wealth is available and accessible to everyone who believes they can make it happen with the right mindset. Refer to this mindset law repeatedly by being "laser focused" from time to time, and you will be wealthy, successful, happy and a nice person to boot!

Do a little more each day. Learn something new and take appropriate action on everything you learn. You cannot go to sleep with the laws that make rich, neither can you pay for it to keep its mouth shut, or give you a head start. What you can do is follow the laws and get attached to thinking about wealth, even when your bank account is empty. Donald Trump was over $1 billion in debt and at his lowest point in life. He made a decision there and then to positively determine a recovery plan and remained focused on such plan in his mindset. Today, the rest is history.

CHOOSE "NOW" TO PURSUE YOUR DESTINY

GOAL

This is where everything is born. Life is a choice of a chosen goal. Everything is a choice. Know what your purpose is for making money. Is it to help your family or for collection of super-cars, or customized clothing, fashionable furniture and handbags? Is it to leave a legacy or to set up a foundation? Is it to grow a large business that can create many jobs? Is it so you can be in a position to teach other people to do the same?

Money is just a consequence of the value you give to other people's lives. How can your purpose add value to the lives of people? When you have real purpose, just as when you are in your 'flow', (your desire and belief becoming a vibrational match), this will radiate and people will get attracted to your vision. Jim Storal's proclamation confirms this, I quote, "nothing is more powerful than a person who knows his destiny and has chosen "now" as the time to pursue it".

Know your purpose and why you are here.

RESOLUTE BELIEF IN YOURSELF REGARDLESS OF ADVERSITIES GETS YOU THERE

CONVICTION

Conviction or faith in ourselves or a higher entity (God) is the second essential ingredient to personal success. It sounds so easy in practice and the truth is that it is, especially if you have a true purpose, a burning desire, passion and belief in yourself and what you do. The case of Colonel Sanders is a living testimony. He was over 65 years old before he discovered the recipe for Kentucky Fried Chicken (KFC). He had faith in himself and his recipe and took the trouble of travelling across America for 2 years, sleeping in his car from restaurant to restaurant, in the hope that someone would like it. Today it has become a historic testimony. You must stop believing in scandalmongers who will always be there to tell you how impossible it is or how everything or everyone is doomed.

Convince yourself that you have everything you need to be all that you can be. Just have that conviction in the wealth you desire and it will come to pass in due season.

THINK ABOUT MONEY A LOT
OF THE TIME OBSESSION

People who have passion and desire in what they do are attractive and successful in their own right, and are generally wealthy and happy. Have passion and desire in everything you do, especially your vocation that creates income, coupled with your investments to make a difference. This includes obsession for money and becoming wealthy. You should be money conscious, money literate and thinking about money a lot of the time.

We get what we focus on most of the time. Footballers do not become the best at their game overnight. They play and train. They have posters of their favorite players. They watch games and study only the best. Only then, when they have gone through the ranks, will they become great players. You need to become money conscious and money focused. You need to know how much you spend to the penny, how much you save, how much you invest and so on. Spend your time with wealthy people, find out what they do, where they go, what they invest in and learn to do the same. Success leaves tracks and in order for you to be where you want to be, you need to follow those tracks. Be passionate and desire the best for yourself.

A HIGH JUMPER JUMPS HIGHER
IF HE RAISES THE BAR

BENCHMARK

Wherever your ceiling of belief is now, you need to raise it. A high jumper only jumps higher if he raises the bar. We get what we believe we can achieve. Our results are directly related to our level of benchmark or belief. Where you are now is relative to your beliefs around money and wealth. What would you say to me if I said you could make 10 times as much as you do now?

If you are not where you want to be right now, then things need to change. Believe that you are always worth far more than you ever get paid. Think in terms of the value you give yourself, your family and other people, and you will always be worth far more than anyone could ever pay you.

Believe in yourself and your ability to attract wealth, and then choose your target beliefs carefully.

THOUGHTS ARE THINGS THAT GIVE ENERGY TO CREATION

PIN-POINT ATTENTION

You get what you focus on, is a basic law that most people find difficult to identify with. Top professional sportsmen are just what they are because they have focused on their sports and being the best for the greatest amount of time, with the highest level of commitment. Anyone who is an expert in their field is not so by accident, but because they have read the most books, done the most studying, had the most learning, made most mistakes and had the most experience.

Thoughts become things. Just think about the idea of flying 500 years ago which the Wright Brothers believed could be done about 400 years thereafter in the twentieth century. They focused on making it happen despite the fact that it had never been done before. If you want to be wealthy, then you must think like the rich. The rich focus on money, wealth, business and so you must learn how to think like them. Find rich people to mentor and coach you. They are where they are because of their focus and you can do and have exactly the same. Learn what you want to know in order to get wealth from those that are already there. Watch yourself grow and compare yourself to you, a year ago for self-assessment.

Be opportunistic and by doing so, you spot more opportunities because, you have a pin-point attention towards your goal.

IT IS NOT ABOUT DECIDING WHEN TO SAY YES, IT IS ABOUT KNOWING WHEN TO SAY NO

DECISION

Both indecisions and over-analysis essentially lead to the same thing; a long road to nowhere! It is good to make many mistakes because it is getting you closer to your goal. Do not fear the consequences of your decisions. Be decisive. Use your knowledge, experience and intuition to make quick and well informed decisions.

Wealthy people do not wait to make decisions; they make decisions and then refine their strategy to improve. The greatest leaders are the most decisive people. It is not just about deciding to say 'yes', it is also about knowing when to say "no". As Napoleon Hill correctly put it "do not wait; time will never be just right". Start where you stand and work with whatever tools you may have at your command and better tools will be found as you go along.

Be a decision maker.

ALWAYS CHECK THE SMALL PRINTS ON ANY CONTRACTS OR AGREEMENTS

THOROUGHNESS

Planning and preparation are absolutely essential to creating wealth and staying successful. Wealthy people are great planners, who give priority attention to diligently strategizing their lives in the areas of finance, investments and career. Know how much you spend weekly, monthly and annually. Know that as a percentage of what you earn. Know how much you save and never touch it, and have a separate account for unexpected costs. Know the accounts that pay the highest interest and know how much tax-free cash you can secure on an annual basis.

Know how much you can afford to risk and know the differences between investing and gambling. Understand risk assessment. Always check the small print on any contract or agreement. Do not believe the first thing you are told on any deals and do not settle for a deal you are not happy with. Read and know how other people have achieved great wealth and success to learn their strategies and psychology.

Be diligent and trust your knowledge, experience and intuition to decide on a strategy.

CONTROL YOUR DESIRES FROM INSTANT GRATIFICATION

DISCIPLINE AND PERSEVERANCE

'Never give up' is a quote from the famous Winston Churchill. This is absolutely essential in a quest for wealth and personal success. It took Thomas Edison thousands of experiments to finally see success in his invention of the incandescent light bulb. He did not give up and did not listen to those who told him that it could not be done. He knew that with every failure he was one step closer to his goals. No one in the world ever thought that the mile could be run in under 4 minutes until Roger Bannister proved the possibility.

Recognize that in every challenge, any failure is a new opportunity and another step closer to your goal. Any journey from where you are to where you want to be will have many twists and turns, road blocks and diversions. That is life. Knowing and really understanding this surely makes life much easier. Just keep on going regardless, and you will reach your goal. Be patient and remain focused on where you are going. Michael Jordan was quoted saying, "I have failed over and over again in my life, and that is why I succeed". Never giving up and having faith in ourselves will send us on our desired path.

If your strategy is to spend 70% of your income, then don't spend any more. This you achieve through an ability to control yourself and your desires from instant gratification.

Be disciplined and stick to your strategy.

UNDERSTAND THE SACRIFICE YOU HAVE TO PAY FOR A PRICE

COMMITMENT

Wealth and success come at a price. What are you prepared to give or give up in order to get to where you want to be? Perhaps it is certain friends, bosses, TV, jobs or environments that hold you back. It is always something. Would you rather give up trashy television and magazines to achieve wealth or give up wealth for a lazy life style? Statistics from Harvard Business School (HBS) reveal that wealthy people start the day early and finish later than the average person. They work harder, longer smarter and more efficiently. They do not choose many hobbies because they are focused. They are disciplined and have a "tunnel vision", understanding the sacrifice they have to make and the price to be paid. They make a determination to be 100% committed to being wealthy.

There is enough money out there for everyone to be a millionaire. Money does not choose where to go and does not discriminate regardless of age, race, creed, culture etc. We can all be rich. If you believe you can be wealthy with an effective strategy and application of the laws (focus, belief, hard work, confidence, commitment, teamwork), you will attract wealth. It is that simple.

TAKE RESPONSIBILITY FOR EVERYTHING IN YOUR LIFE

LEADERSHIP

Do you know anybody who is always blaming other people for the things that go wrong? People who always blame the boss, the weather or bad luck for their misfortunes? This is not the attitude of the wealthy and successful who understand responsibility. The performance of their business is not due to market movements, but to diligence, focus and persistence in following the laws they learned and practiced. When things go wrong or challenges arise, they will be the first to throw up their hand and take full responsibility.

When there is success, they lay all the plaudits to the members of their team. This is Leadership by example. You will be amazed of how empowering this attitude is, in getting so much from those around you, who feel inspired by success and not blamed for failure. The more you take responsibility for everything in your life, the more you will be in control of the things that happen in your life.

TRUST YOURSELF AND WHAT YOUR SUBCONSCIOUS TELLS YOU

INSTINCTS AND INTUITIONS

Everything you have ever learned or experienced has been "stored" in your subconscious. You have an innate ability to think about any situation by processing pieces of information in milliseconds without thinking. This is instinct and intuition at work. Trust yourself and what your subconscious tells you.

You will be right to listen to yourself always. Trust is everything in life; in business, in wealth and in relationships with other people. When you find people you can trust along the road of your life, hold on to them. If they are employees, reward them, treat them like gold, as if they are family. Trust your instincts and intuitions and live with your decisions.

Believe in your instincts to make the right decision now.

RAISE THE BAR OF YOUR THINKING LIKE DONALD TRUMP

PROJECT WEALTH

If you want to be wealthy and attract money, you need to believe you have the ability and unique qualities to attract it. Projecting wealth is the key to this. If you look wealthy, people will think you are wealthy and that will attract wealth and wealthy people to you. The clothes you wear and how you present yourself, the way you hold yourself and body language are all paramount to your success at attracting wealth. Project confidence, power and inner calm, just like those who have made it and made it big.

If you want more money, think bigger deals and increase your level of belief. If you want bigger results as a real estate business man, start looking at towers and skyscrapers and not one-bedroom flat property. Take a queue from Donald Trump to raise your bar of thinking. Duncan Bennatyne started with one ice cream van and now controls over $250 million. Daniel Pena started with a phone and $800 and grew to a $6 billion oil company.

Gradually expand your thinking and belief, and your results will get bigger and better.

NO SUCH THING AS STANDING STILL

ACCEPT CHANGE

If living things are not growing, they are dying. In this world there is actually no such thing as standing still. It is either forwards or backwards. Growth, evolution of the self, and the acceptance that things do not stay the same are so important to your mindset for the achievement of wealth and success. The arrival of the internet for example has made it possible to access any information about creation in the palm of your hands! It was an unimaginable feat to contemplate 50 years ago. Many people have lived life in a certain way and are resistant to change. It is counterproductive and such a waste of energy. Those who do not stay up to date with the fast moving world get left behind. They die.

Your wealth and success is dependent on growth. It is not just accepting the things that are new but growing within one's self. Your needs will change over time. A lot will depend on your age, exposure, education and emotion. The people you know and deal with will change, society will change, the rates and banks and the value of money will change. The way you spend money will change.

Understand this very important concept and accept it. Revise your strategy as you feel the need, because growth and change are part of your journey.

DO NOT BE A SLAVE. THINK OUT OF THE BOX

SHEEP OR SHEPHERD

If we do what everyone else does, we will get the same result as everyone else. Most people are not wealthy, independent or in a position of choice in their life. Most people are living in effect rather than at cause (they are slaves), and do not know what to do. It is very important to be strong, to stick to your strategy and question the advice you are getting from someone, especially if it is from the typical conservative minded person whose opinion is taken from the tabloid.

When there is property 'crash' the sheep flock and sell and lose money. The ones that succeed are the ones that have a strategy and are confident about such strategy. In this case they will buy and hold when everyone is selling. The ones that succeed are usually different, courageous, focused, creative, perhaps stubborn, and decisive. The rest are just like crabs that will not get out of the box or allow another crab to get out.

You have to be courageous to be successful and not act like a sheep or crab.

ADD VALUE TO PEOPLE'S LIVES

MONEY OBJECTIVE

Think back to your purpose. Do you want wealth to change the world or create a higher standard of living for you and your loved ones? Do you want to set up a shelter or charity? Do you want a specific thing, to travel to certain places or to flaunt your fashionable acquisitions?

It is good to write down your goal or checklist as a reminder or reference to look back to see the progress you have made. Remember that money is just a consequence of what we do. However, it is better to act as if money is not as important as the good you do for other people, and the value you add to their lives. When you act this way, you will be in a good place to attract more of money than you ever had before. Know exactly what you want your money for.

Add value to people's lives and think about justice, safety, fairness, value and legacy when you are attracting wealth.

LIFE IS A JOURNEY, NOT A DESTINATION

FUTURE PATHWAY PLAN

You get to think about the things you want most in your life and it will be attracted to you. You need to have the skill of seeing your journey before you. This involves the following process.

1. Where are you now? This may sound ridiculous, but many people could be described as 'delusional' when it comes to knowing where they are. However you should evaluate where you are and get excited about the path you are about to build.
2. Know where you want to go. What is it you want? Is it financial independence, more income, super cars, private jet, etc? Because life is a journey and not a destination. Each major goal will act as a significant milestone in your life. Be specific with time scales about your goal.
3. Be a man with a strategy. Do you want to build an empire or a legacy?

Bear in mind also that it is never too late and you are never too young to set your goals. Now is always the best time. Stay focused, aware and ready to see your journey before you.

BE A KING OF THE SPREADSHEET, PRINCE OF PROJECTION

‒‒‒‒‒‒ ◦◦◦◦◦◦ ‒‒‒‒‒‒

START A STRATEGY

Most people live life by accident. You must develop a strategy which becomes your road map to follow and update when necessary. You must set up a strategy starting from where you are now in the sequence.

1.   Know how much you spend. You need to be the king of the spread sheet, prince of projection and budgeting, and to know exactly how much you have to spend.

     Know your attitude to risks. How much you are ready to risk or speculate in your investment strategy.

2.   Know your potential sources of income particularly about passive income.
3.   Cash flow and capital growth.

     Understand the difference.

4.   Think about where you are going to donate your TITHE. You must also save a percentage of your

income and never touch it. This is an enabling strategy that will make you very wealthy at the end of your life.

Make your strategy renewable every year.

FACTOR FLEXIBILITY INTO YOUR CONTINGENCY PLANS

WORSE-CASE SCENARIO

Things will always take longer than you think, be harder and more challenging than you think and cost more than you think. This is a fact of business and a fact of life.

In every business proposition or plan, you must always think and take into account the worst case scenario. If you plan your business to be making profit in 3 years and do not happen until year 5, what are you going to do? How would you survive? You must work your sensitivity analysis (projections of earnings and turnover), based on figures that are low. If you budget $10,000 for marketing, think more $15,000 or $20,000 because things always end up costing more, especially when they take longer. There will always be the unexpected costs that will sting you if you have not factored them in a good contingency plan.

Keep a close eye on your money because they are plenty of ways that it can be taken from you.

Always think of the worse-case scenario.

WHERE IS YOUR FIRE ESCAPE? FIND IT

KNOW YOUR EXIT

Before you walk into any bar you should know where the fire escape is. We should look carefully at how we can get out and liquidate efficiently and cost effectively.

Absolutely check all the small print to anything you sign and make sure you know the contract. Never sign anything unless you absolutely know what you are signing and how you can exit safely and cost efficiently.

Sometimes knowing when to get out can be as important as knowing when to get in.

NO MAN IS AN ISLAND UNTO HIMSELF

TEAM WORK

Just as quoted by Napoleon Hill, "it takes team-work to make the dream work". This is because no man is an island onto himself. We all need great people around us: friends, family, coaches, mentors and advisors to help us grow and help in areas that we are not as strong. The amount of money that you can make will directly correlate to the amount of value you can give to other people. If you can add some kind of value to other people's lives, then you will always be wealthy and abundant.

Anything from a smile that can make their day, to financial offering and opportunity and everything in between. The greatest leaders in the business world may look like they achieve success on their own, but that is not the case. Richard Branson could not have built Virgin Mobile without Freddie Laker and Microsoft would not be in force for Bill Gates without Paul Allen supporting him.

The real key is to build strong and trusting relationships with others and to find ways in which you can help them and add value to their lives. It is said that contact between 7 people can give you access to everyone on the planet!

Treat everyone well and build a strong network of great people around you.

UNDERSTAND THE
LANGUAGE OF MONEY

∽∽∾∽

FINANCIAL LITERACY

Consistent practice and knowledge of the rules is the only way we are going to achieve wealth and success.

It is all very well being great at visualization and manifestation, but without knowledge and doing something about it, nothing will ever be done.

It is necessary to use consistent action with never-ending improvement and you will be as wealthy as you believe you can be.

By the same yard stick, if you want to be wealthy, then you need to be able to speak the language of money. The language that we use is a direct representation of the knowledge we have on the subject of money. The list is exhaustive, but basically, you must be familiar with reading balance sheets, understanding the lifetime values of your charts, know your net worth, sensitivity analysis, running costs, difference between assets and liability, financial book and management etc.

Improve your financial language, improve your knowledge, improve your results and improve your wealth.

MAKE YOUR MONEY WORK FOR YOU THROUGH TEAM WORK

LEVERAGE

Leverage is utilizing other people's time, money and skill-set, to gain greater advantage, result or wealth, than you could ever do on your own. You can use leverage in many different ways and it is advisable to always think in terms of leverage by getting other people to do the things you cannot do. Your ability to leverage and attract wealth and success will rely upon being a great leader, who can offer great benefits as follows:

1. Never ridicule someone who is learning.
2. Only reprimand in private if necessary.
3. Always praise good work publicly.
4. Be personable and care about other people.
5. Remunerate good work financially.
6. Motivate, inspire and lead by example.
7. Be consistent.
8. Forgive.
9. Write down the outcome before you start.
10. Set realistic goals, set others for success

Make your money and your wealth work for you and be constantly looking to leverage.

BUILD YOUR WEALTH ON SOLID FINANCIAL AND EDUCATIONAL FOUNDATION

SUSTAINABILITY AND MODELLING

Rome was not built in a day, nor was nearly all of the wealthy people and families on the planet earth. In every career, business or investment, it is good to ascertain if it is sustainable over a long term period or if it can create a good return on investment.

Warren Buffet (owns 50% of Coca-Cola shares), looks for stocks that have longevity and sustainability, and you should be doing the same for your education, career, business and investment.

Build your wealth steady and over time on a solid financial and educational foundation. Think long term and you will be forever wealthy for generations to come.

It is strongly advisable that you make a life mission, to seek those who have what you want and learn from them. Read books about wealthy and successful people you admire. Hunt them down and buy them lunch. Take them out and ask them how they did it. They will be happy to share their experiences with you. Their success becomes a track for you to learn from and replicate.

BE FLEXIBLE, PROFESSIONAL, AND PERSONAL WHEN NEGOTIATING

NEGOTIATION AND BORROWING

Think cooperation not competition. Think partnership and long term benefits to building great relationships.

Negotiation is prevalent everywhere, not just in your job, business, wealth and success. It will make you better with your kids, family, friends and loved ones.

Know your goal, what you want from the deal and what other people want from the deal. Be flexible, professional and personal. In the case of borrowing, you must endeavor to avoid the following:

1. Only ever borrow from friends and family if you absolutely must.
2. Only borrow to invest in income producing assets.
3. Never borrow to invest in liabilities.
4. Think very carefully when you are compelled to borrow. Only ever borrow if you have to.

YOU CAN ENRICH AND AWAKEN BILLIONS OF PEOPLE OUT OF FINANCIAL SLUMBER

PASS-ON THE TORCH

What could be your give back policy? Would it be to give your inheritance to your children and grandchildren in a way that would educate them for their future business and careers? Could it be a case of passing on to foundations that use it wisely for the benefit of other less fortunate?

One should take a lead from Bill and Melinda Gates foundation and from Warren Buffet. Look how we can help others in a way that will empower them to have a life of choice that we chose for ourselves. We need to give value to other peoples' lives while we are alive, so why not do the same when we go? It will be expedient to seek counsel from a financial advisor. The feeling of giving back will add huge value to our lives.

On the other hand you might feel good to be wealthy and successful which is a good feeling. It feels better however to pass on the knowledge to help others achieve the same.

Success breeds success while wealth attracts wealth. A life becomes so much more abundant by thousands of times over when the knowledge is shared. It's not just about giving money, it is about giving Education.

Think of the fun we can teach our kids about the laws of wealth and success, teaching our friends and family, using the internet to teach thousands of others. We can even increase our wealth substantially by doing so.

Pass on the knowledge about wealth creation and you will be Enriching and Awakening millions/billions of people out of Financial Slumber!

These are the Recipes for Unlimited Success, tried and tested successfully by the very rich over many generations. If this Template is correctly applied, then you are unquestionably on the road to becoming a Money Magnet.

REMAIN IN ROBUST HEALTH

Your wealth will lead to sorrow if you have a bad health. It confirms the ancient proverb that says "health is wealth". Good health is only attainable through self-discipline by taking-in the right combination of nutrients. The fact remains that as cultures differ among various nationalities, so do the types of acceptable dieting apply, as standards of such people. It will therefore be impossible to recommend a globally acceptable standard-dieting formula. However, there is a common denominator about the nutritional value that the body needs to remain robust and healthy, regardless of wherever the food is produced. What this means is that value should be placed on quality of nutritional content, rather than quantity of any food consumed by anyone.

THE PERFECT FOOD MORINGA OLEIFERA

Regardless of what anyone wants to consume as food, an attempt is made in this book to develop a new mindset for using natural and globally-recognized food-plants. The one that stands out as "first among equals" is MORINGA OLEIFERA, an ancient plant universally recognized, over 4000 years ago. It has been processed into powdered palatable state of consumption and classified as a perfect food. It is produced in the USA by Zija International from the State of Utah. Zija is the only company to deliver Moringa in such convenient and natural 100% blend, using the most nutrient rich parts of the tree, the leaves, seeds, trunk, to stand above the pack of comparative manufacturers. Empirical research has proclaimed Moringa with the following comparative advantages:

1. 4 times the Calcium of Milk.
2. 4 times the Vitamin A of Carrots.
3. 3 times the Potassium of Bananas.
4. 4 times the Protein of Yogurt.
5. 7 times the Vitamin C of Oranges.
6. 3 times the Iron of Spinach.
7. 3 times the Vitamin E of Almonds.

Within 14 days of using Moringa, you will begin to notice Amazing Improvements to your health status from this ancient plant. By the authority of the USA National Institute of Health and Medicine, UN World Food Program, and National Science Foundation, Moringa can "arrest, reverse and cure over 300 diseases and disorders", ranging from HIV, Diabetes, High/Low-Blood Pressure, Cancer, Liver Disease, Skin Disease, Arthritis, Overweight, Cardiac Function etc. It was declared the 2007 MVP champion of the plant world which is confirmable on Discovery Channel. In the area of energy, Moringa Energy Drink is second-to-none in its natural effect on your health. This is just a summary of the Moringa story, and every reader is advised to partake in this PERFECT FOOD! Check www.soltan.myzija.com for more details or read the book "Moringa, Myth or Miracle" by Dr Howard Fisher, author of over 15 books.

TESTIMONY

My daughter Olufemi was afflicted with Anaemia for over 20 years and tried all kinds of medications recommended by medical specialists to no avail. When I came across Moringa, I decided to try it on my daughter who at that time was 27 years old. Within 4 weeks of using Moringa, she felt a world of improvement and decided to consult her Doctor. The test that was carried out showed total elimination of Anaemia from her body. To this day, she is Free of the sickness for good.

RECEIVE THE TREASURES OF LIFE

"We are Organo Gold and this is who we are"

Coffee is the most consumed Beverage after Water and the second Most Traded Commodity after Oil. People drink coffee all day everyday around the world. The Big Question is to ask yourself when was the last time you got Paid because someone enjoyed a cup of coffee? Popular Franchises realize the benefits of the large market in Coffee Consumption, such that you can now offer billions of drinkers a better choice to earn money every time other people drink coffee.

Organo Gold coffee is blended with Ganoderma. For over 4000 years, Ganoderma has been recognized as the highest-ranked of all Herbs that assures a long life, among many other cures. It works to detox and rejuvenate the body to strengthen the immune system, reduce cholesterol, increase oxygen, as well as lifting your spirit! As if that were not enough, it also balances your blood sugar levels, improves pancreatic functions with capacity of controlling destruction of healthy cells and more!

This is what Organo Gold stands for. Organo Gold is on a mission, spreading the knowledge of Ganoderma to the four corners of the world. By using the cost effective network distribution system to deliver these Ganoderma products, more of every dollar is shared with our growing Organo Gold family world-wide.

Think about your future. Where will you and your family be in 5 years from right now? You may know where you want to be, but do you know how you are going to get there? Do you have a plan? Now more than ever it's up to you to define your future. That's where Organo Gold comes into the picture.

Organo Gold is a global family that is growing and thriving every day. A family that is caring and compassionate and believes that the knowledge of Ganoderma should be in the hands of people world-wide. It's a family that cares about you.

Organo Gold blends the unequalled power of Ganoderma with an unparalleled business opportunity that will allow you to capitalize in the ever expanding health and wellness industry. By positioning your Organo Gold business in front of worldwide aging trends, it can be as big and successful as you want it to be. Whether it's improved health, more time freedom or better wealth, Organo Gold can help you achieve your goals. As an independent Organo Gold entrepreneur we put you first.

Imagine living a life of health, abundance and freedom. Just imagine having access to products with the power of Ganoderma. Imagine how huge the world-wide market for these products can be. And now just think of how that can affect you. The Organo Gold execution plan, our world-wide distribution system combined with the power of Ganoderma all add up to perfect timing.

Organo Gold is about the empowerment of individuals through the strength of team work. Organo Gold's industry leading compensation plan makes everything possible. It's an innovative and generous plan that will reward you for leadership and commitment. The power of Organo Gold has already created incomes that have been life changing. It can change your life too.

The business of Organo Gold can be compared to a franchise with Starbucks Coffee but this time around, with a far better comparative advantage by way of quick significant returns. It is all about sharing and improving lives of people and making money in the process.

Consider the fact that coffee is the largest traded commodity next to oil. Imagine yourself being positioned in the midst of this massive movement, to enable you help people get richer and healthier, while equally enriching yourself without leaving your home! In addition, you are given the liberty of choice to adopt any or all of seven (7) different ways of generating amazing income from its Compensation Program at www. glitterglowrich.myorganogold.com.

OXYGEN THERAPY IS A LIVE-WIRE

This is a universally-certified research result with some exciting breakthrough news regarding Cancer and all other diseases. This information is in regards to Oxygen and how you can quickly have 12 times more Oxygen going through your bloodstream and reaching every cell in your body. This was scientifically documented at a major University in Utah.

It has been discovered that diseases cannot exist in the presence of high levels of Oxygen.

There is a doctor (name withheld), who now lives out of the USA because his life was being threatened as a result of the amazing recoveries his patients were experiencing. He had a clinic in Arizona where he treated people from all over the country.

His latest and most effective therapy was in combining together enough Oxygen Generators to produce ten cubic feet of oxygen per minute. (Less than this amount did not produce results) He had his patients breathe pure oxygen deeply while exercising for fifteen minutes. Note: There are some dangers, so do not try this without the help of someone who is trained in this kind of therapy.

Typically, these patients saw immediate improvement and within two weeks, many diseases had completely disappeared along with their associated pain. He confirmed that his patients were starting to look like they had received a face lift. This therapy however, was rather costly and people had to physically visit his office in order to use it. Now they have to travel outside of the country in order to take this therapy, which many people still do.

A world-renowned Consultant Certified Nutritionist was introduced to this new method by a certified trainer, nutritionist and natural healer. She is the founder and developer of this method of breathing, which provides all of the benefits that the patients of the doctor on exile were receiving and even more. This is a 5-minute therapy that can be done once daily (or multiple times for faster results) in the comfort of your own home and you will start seeing results starting the very first day.

For example, one 95 year old Cancer patient was curled up in a fetal position in excruciating pain and was so close to death that her eyes were glazed over. She needed help to even start the therapy, but she began responding with the very first treatment. Within 2 weeks she was up, taking care of herself and went on to experience a full recovery.

This therapy was tested independently by scientists at the University of Utah. The published reports say that people who are overweight will experience twenty one times (21) the weight loss they would receive as a result of intensive weight training. This therapy was shown to burn as much as 7,000 calories in one workout. One person lost seven pounds from one session because of the increased calorie burn over a 24-hour period.

On the other hand, many people, including some cancer patients need to gain weight. This therapy will build six times (6) more lean muscle and also increase bone density faster than intensive weight training. People who have tried to gain weight without success can now see muscle tissue and weight return to normal.

Those suffering from Osteoporosis and weak bones will also see their bone density and strength return. As a testimony to strong bones, there was a 61-year-old man who fell from the roof of his new home he was building and landed directly on a metal beam, hip first. Most people would have suffered a broken hip from such a fall, but not a single bone was broken. He did suffer some nerve damage, but thanks to the grace of God, good supplements and these breathing exercises, he fully and was completely healed.

Previous clients have said that it completely eliminated Cancer, Leukemia, Emphysema, COPD, Asthma, Sleep Apnea, Chronic Pain, completely regenerate blackened smokers lung, made them look and feel years younger, gave them instant and lasting energy and made them sleep better.

This therapy also produces 12 times more flexibility than Yoga and Martial Arts Training. But what is most exciting to many people is the fact that it takes away wrinkles and makes you look and feel years younger. It is believed that the "youthing" effect is due to the fact that this therapy naturally increases and balances the body's hormone levels.

Another important thing is how quickly this exercise produces endorphins. Endorphins are endogenous opioid peptides that function as neurotransmitters. They are produced by the pituitary gland and the hypothalamus in vertebrates during exercise and they resemble opiates in their ability to produce analgesia and a feeling of well-being.

These brain chemicals bring feelings of calmness and tranquility and are natural pain killers. They help increase circulation; help the body to heal faster and give and overall sense of well-being. Endorphins also give you a sense of power and control over problems and situations.

The endorphin rush that is experienced from long distance running and aerobic workouts is greatly desirable, so much so that millions of people perform strenuous physical exercises daily to achieve what is commonly referred to as the "runners high."

With one simple exercise, you can produce more endorphins in 5-minutes than you can produce in 5-miles of running. The beauty is you can do this exercise anytime you feel like you need a boost in energy, mental clarity or control over some problem.

If you fully understood the benefits of endorphins alone, you would take the necessary few minutes each day to perform this workout.

OXYGEN is the Spark of Life and just as a fire can't burn without oxygen, our cells can't produce heat and energy without oxygen. Oxygen is extracted from the air we breathe by the lungs. It passes into the blood vessels that surround the lungs and is carried to all the cells of the body by the blood. Most of the oxygen is carried by the red blood cells, although the water in the blood carries some of it and a deficiency of water means reduced oxygen delivery by the blood. Oxygen is so important, that even where optimum water, protein, vitamin and mineral intake exists, ill health will still exist if there is an oxygen deficiency.

Oxygen levels in the atmosphere are believed to have been as high as 50% at one time. Today the oxygen level is about 20% and will continue to drop as major rain forests continue to be cut down and reduced oxygen levels are a major cause of disease.

Unfortunately most people breathe shallowly and under-breathing is epidemic among adults, which is another major cause of oxygen deficiency in adults.

Shallow breathing is often related to stress, and tight clothing coupled with a lifetime of rushing to and fro, sitting hunched over desks and working or playing on computers produces stress.

The mechanics of breathing determines oxygen supply. Shallow chest breathing gives rise to oxygen deficiencies, as there are very few blood vessels surrounding the upper lobes of the lungs. Most of the blood vessels are found in the lower lobes of the lung, so deep, abdominal breathing is the answer to optimum oxygen levels.

Babies and drunks don't chest breathe. They're both so relaxed that they breathe easily and deeply and their tummies rise and fall to the rhythm of their breathing. Shallow chest breathing is a bad habit we develop as we move towards adulthood. However it is a habit that can easily be unlearned by practicing deep breathing exercises and by slowing down.

If you want to burn lots of calories or build muscle, then you will want to combine some form of strenuous exercise or weight training with the breathing exercises.

You may think that you need a video or a coach to show you how to do these exercises correctly, but that is not the case. You will however want to read the following section again before doing the exercises repeatedly, because you will pick up little points each time you read these instructions that will improve the results you will receive. There are two ways to do the exercise but the more convenient one recommended here is the "Horse Shoe" method compared to laying flat.

To get the feeling of how to breathe correctly, lay flat on your back and imagine a nose connected to the back of your spine directly opposite, or slightly below your belly button. Put one hand on your chest and the other hand on your abdomen. Imagine breathing in through the nose connected to your spine and then take a large breath as quickly as you can. Your abdomen should rise, but your chest should not move.

Practice breathing in this manner until it becomes natural and until you can do so without a lot of mental effort.

You can actually do the breathing part sitting on a chair with your back erect. However you will burn a lot more calories if you add some muscle burn to the breathing. You can combine the breathing with any kind of strenuous exercise, but perhaps the best exercise for the largest number of people is what we call the "horse stance" in martial arts.

The horse stance exercises the largest muscle group in the legs and burns a lot of calories quickly. A person, for example, that is practiced in Tai Chi can go outside, scantily dressed in cold weather and by simply standing in a horse stance will soon have sweat rolling off their brow.

To begin with, stand with your feet shoulder width (or slightly more) apart. Your feet should be parallel or even slightly pigeon toed. Next lower your butt toward the floor as if you were sitting on a horse. At all times keep your back straight, or in other words do not lean forward.

This is not a competition, so do what is comfortable for you. You will however quickly notice some burning sensation in your legs because you are exercising muscles you don't normally use. Ignore the pain as it will pay some great dividends in the end. In time, you will be able to squat lower and burn more calories even faster.

While standing in the horse stance, exhale all of the air in your lungs. Again, you are going to be exercising some new muscles and with time these muscles will grow stronger, which means that you will increase the oxygen levels in your lungs and blood 24-hours a day.

After forcing out all of the air you can possibly exhale, imagine having been underwater for 3 minutes and you are about to expire and you finally get your head above water; you are going to suck in the air with all of the force you can muster. In this manner breathe in through your nose and fill the lungs to capacity. If you inhale with enough force, it will partially close off the nose opening and may even cause the nose to rattle, like a child snuffing his or her nose.

As you practice doing this daily, your lungs will grow much stronger and you will be able to inhale even more forcefully. The amount of force you use when inhaling is "directly" proportional to the amount of oxygen you will be putting into your blood stream. It is also proportional to the amount of endorphins your body will produce. If done correctly, you can produce more endorphins in 5-minutes of breathing than you can produce in a 5-mile run.

The endorphins produced by breathing will stay with you a lot longer, because when running, your body produces uric acid, which in less than two hours will neutralize all of the endorphins that you may have produced while running.

If you are suffering from any kind of pain, you will want all of the endorphins you can get, because not only are they a powerful pain killer, they also help the body to heal faster than any other natural substance.

Now your lungs are filled with every drop of air that you could possibly suck in. Hold your breath as long as you can. In the beginning, this may only be for a short time, but as your lungs grow stronger, your ability to hold longer will greatly increase. This is a sign that your lungs are growing much stronger.

When you are ready to exhale, press your lips tightly together, so as to make it more difficult to exhale. Now blow hard like you are blowing a trumpet or trying to blow up a balloon. When you have exhaled approximately one third of your air, open your mouth as wide as you can and force the remaining air out of your lungs.

Coughing while exhaling the last two thirds of the air from your lungs will also be helpful as it exercises your diaphragm and also strengthens your heart. Tighten every muscle in your lungs and abdomen and force out every drop of air that you possibly can. This will burn toxins and fat and get them out of your body faster than any other detox program and this form of detoxification will not make you sick the same as many others will.

Now that your lungs are completely empty, close off the mouth and nose and try to breathe in. This will create a vacuum in your lungs and when done correctly, you will notice that your diaphragm and the soft tissue around your Adam's apple will cave in slightly from the vacuum created.

This vacuum will cause all kinds of toxins and gases to be pulled out of the surrounding tissues into the lungs, where they will be burned and exhaled on the succeeding cycle of breathing.

This completes one cycle of breathing and the goal is to work up to five complete cycles per session. If you are a beginner, you may want to stop at this point and just do one cycle at a time three or more times throughout the day. Just one set of five cycles will greatly increase oxygen to your blood and cells and step up your metabolism for faster weight gain. Those who are serious about improving health, losing weight or increasing muscle mass will to do three or more sets of these exercises daily.

After exhaling and holding your breath in a vacuum as long as you comfortably can, you can either rest by breathing normally for a few breaths, or you can go directly into the second cycle by breathing in to capacity with all of the force you can muster.

Beginners will find it difficult to go directly into the second cycle without resting, but as your lungs grow stronger, you will eventually be able to do 5 cycles in a row with no problem.

After completing the 5 cycles, you will have more oxygen in your blood than you have had for years. If you are an athlete in training or you just want to go to the next level in fitness or weight loss, you can at this time do your weight training, pushups, yoga, martial arts, etc. You will notice an increase in strength, repetitions, flexibility and endurance.

One person used this form of training to win first place in a triathlon without running, swimming or cycling as part of their preparation.

Recap:

Stand in a horse stance

Exhale all of the air in your lungs through your mouth

Inhale to capacity with all of the force you can possibly muster

Hold as long as you comfortably can

Blow out the first third of your air through lips that are tightly held together

Open the mouth wide and force out all of the remaining air while coughing

Seal the airway and try to breathe in creating a vacuum

Hold as long as you comfortably can

Either relax and breathe normally for a short time or go directly into the second round of breathing exercise

Work up to five cycles per session

Repeat 3 or more times later in the day for maximum result

Many people will start coughing up a lot of phlegm, which is merely the body now getting enough oxygen to start the detoxification of the body. In time the lungs will clear up and other problems will also begin to disappear.

More oxygen in your blood will begin to turn around every single health challenge you might have because disease cannot live in the presence of oxygen. A health consultant of repute has helped over 1,000 people recover from cancer naturally and increasing oxygen levels was a major part of the program.

These exercises are an integral part of regaining and maintaining perfect health and should be practiced daily accompanied by proper diet, supplements and increased fluid intake in the form of pure water, because oxygen alone does not provide the other necessary building blocks that create a healthy, beautiful body. Oxygen only allows them to accomplish their individual roles within the cells.

Visit: www.healthyventura.com

Headache Natural Cure

Breathing Therapy: The nose has a left and a right nostril. Although we use both to inhale and exhale, they each have a different functions. Some cultures have long recognized this fact and have used the symbol of the sun to represent the right nostril and the moon to represent the left nostril.

During a headache, close your right nostril and use your left nostril to breathe.

In about 5 minutes, your headache will be gone. If you feel tired, just reverse, close your left nostril and breathe through your right nostril. After a few minutes you will feel your mind will feel refreshed.

Right side belongs to 'hot', so it gets heated up easily and left side belongs to 'cold'.

Most females breathe with their left nostrils, so they get "cooled off" faster.

Most of the guys breathe with their right nostrils, they get worked up.

You may begin to pay attention the moment you wake up to see which nostril is more open and thus takes in air faster. If the left is faster, you will feel tired. So, close your left nostril and use your right nostril for breathing, you will feel refreshed quickly.

This can be taught to children, but it is more effective when practiced by adults.

A college student suffered with headaches literally every night and she took prescription pain killers from her doctor, but they didn't really help. Her studies and grades suffered as a result of the headaches.

She then heard about this breathing therapy and decided to try it. She closed her right nostril and breathed through her left nostril for five minutes. In less than a week, her headaches were gone!

Headaches have an underlying problem with toxins in the body. The exercise above no doubt helps to burn toxins out of the brain by providing more oxygen. However, to speed up the process of burning toxins and also to provide a whirlwind of oxygen to all of the cells of the body, go back to the breathing exercise again.

Headaches are also usually associated with stomach problems. Ginger spice is one of the best things to calm an upset stomach and take care of a headache. Make ginger tea for yourself whenever you have an upset stomach or headache, which almost always takes care of the problem.

Alternatively, mix ¼-½ teaspoon-full of powered ginger in a cup of warm water two times a day to see the difference it makes.

The Breathing Technique and Headache Cure are vital samples of what Natural Cures can do. It also confirms that Natural Nutrients change your body terrain in cell vibration, energy production, detoxification and many other health benefits faster and naturally. It is the lack of the minerals they produce that manifest as diseases (lack-of-ease) in the Body!

For more enquiries on any solution required concerning Natural Cures, visit www.joytolive.info.

EXTRAORDINARY HEALING
POWER OF LAMININE

—◦◦◦◦—

Laminine is the Light that brings Life to your Body Cells.
By Anonymous

This is the beginning of the Best Part Of Your Life, for experiencing anew, a Supernatural Adaptogen!

Accolades should go to the pioneer of this Miracle-Medical- Breakthrough from the early twentieth century in Canada by name Dr John Davidson. He found an antidote to cancer which successfully cured many patients, but was denied recognition and support by the government of the day, for some inexplicable reasons. Over time however, this Historic Feat turned out to become an irony of fate because, many decades after his death, his work was revisited by renowned experts and institutions to corroborate its authenticity. The result of further research on Dr Davidson's discovery gave birth to a product known as Laminine.

Laminine is a stem-cell- miracle- technology of unprecedented potential. It is a combination of extracts from the following:

Shark Cartilage
Green Pea Protein Extract
Nine(9)- Day Old Protein Extract from Egg.

Laminine combination is an Adaptogen that activates stem-cells into action. They are known to contain Protein Extracts, loaded with Fibroblast- Growth- Factor (FGF), acting as signal molecules to inform dormant stem-cells into reactivation, to all parts of the body. FGF is a compound glue- protein exclusively available in adults, essential to supporting embryonic developments that give life to dead cells. It is the Mother of All Health Solution Inventions, which can be likened to a software programme, facilitating life, to any dormant component of a computer.

Laminine is the food for the stem-cell with a capacity to control the nutritional bank balance of Neurotransmitters and Hormones, which make up the Ruling Class of your body. It is the Cellular Molecule holding the body together, to instruct the repair and regeneration of damaged cells back to life, with profound rejuvenating effect and Speed. It brings the body to balance. Under two (2) weeks of using this adaptogen, you begin to observe startling results.

The unprecedented benefits of this Natural Synergistic Super- Food, not only balances your Neurotransmitters and Hormones. It also allows the Brain create its adult stem-cells to proceed, in rejuvenating any part of the body that requires Healing. The body has its own healing mechanism and so, Laminine allows the body to diagnose itself for balancing deficiencies in blood sugar, cholesterol, serotonin, depression, fear, AIDs, cancer, arthritis, kidney failure, diabetes, eyesight, etc, or deficiencies to just any other ailment in the body.

The Best Part of Your Life is just beginning when you decide to use Laminine Adaptogen in your routine dieting regime. There will be remarkable reduction in your cortisol and stress hormones to enliven your spirit as a starting experience. It can be likened to the Power of Resurrection, activating all dormant cells of the body to get excited once again! Imagine a Protein Molecule that balances deficiencies in all endocrine and hormones like Brain Homeostasis, Blood Sugar, Cholesterol, Serotonin all in one go.

Laminine is a fundamental protein that enables the body structure to "hold together", found in the extra-cellular matrix that form the engine room of all internal organs. It looks like a cross, composed of chains coiling around each other to control all neurotransmitters and hormones of the body. Page 133 of this book explains most of these medical terminologies.

Empirical testimonials around the world attest to 100% efficacy of Laminine, though its effect may vary in relation to the appropriate dosage required of an individual, or the degree of your peculiar medical history. They all come with the same positive results without exception. I am a living witness to attest to the tremendous overall improvements of health within ten days of trial, that made all pains and ailments miraculously disappear. In addition, imagine yourself to budget less than $50 per month to be" free at last" of Health Complaints by this supernatural supplement.

Contact email soltansecurity@hotmail.com or visit www. mylifepharm.com/glowrich to get enriched, when you decide to enrol as a distributor or preferred consumer. Check the incredible testimonials about Laminine on any internet outlet to see outstanding experiences. It is a window of opportunity that turns into a testimony, coupled with connecting with a promising business fortune, to prosper beyond pressure.

RECOMMENDATIONS

The following Eating and Sporting Habits must be cultivated for good health:

1. Eat food that is as close to nature's growth cycle as possible. Let Moringa become part of your Daily Diets.
2. Eat organically grown produce.
3. Eat fresh organic vegetables.
4. Eat organically grown grains such as rice, barley and buckwheat.
5. Eat organically grown beef, chicken, lamb and veal.
6. Eat three meals a day.
7. Eat fresh fruits and vegetables every day.
8. Stay away from artificial sweeteners, high fructose corn syrup, mono sodium glutamate, and harmful chemicals and additives.
9. Counter balance nutritional deficiencies.
10. Take whole food supplements.
11. Remove Toxins by doing cleanses of your colon, liver, kidney etc
12. Protect yourself from Electromagnetic Frequencies of cell phones, TV, cell towers by using eliminators.

13. Read uplifting and positively inspiring books every day.

Do physical exercises by walking for one hour, look at things far away, jog, stand on a vibration plate, etc.

UNIVERSITY OF HARD-KNOCKS

This is the story of a young man who left his country of origin in search of the Golden Fleece in the new found land of the United States of America. He gained admission into a top university to study medicine, but quit school after two years, inspite of the high grades he made.

For the next couple of years, he took jobs where ever he was accepted, and found himself working in more than ten different places in a very short time. This experience bothered him to the point of determination, never to seek employment anymore, but rather work for himself. With little savings and loan from few friends, he was able to buy a car with which to run a car-hire service. Things appeared to work well for a while until suddenly, the business crashed with no cash in hand.

The last resort was for him to live on welfare and food-stamps which he found most depressing and humiliating. Unknown to him, that became the turning point of his life, when he ran into an old friend at a social church fellowship. His friend was doing well in international trading business, and so decided to let Samsom share in the knowledge of the business.

Out of desperation to make a success of his life, Samson decided within himself that enough was enough. He was prepared to go the extra mile at whatever he did, and that meant a decision to talk to anyone who cared to listen. He weathered the storm with tireless energy, never to give up on any deal, no matter the threat of failure, defeat or disappointment that came his way. This was one attitude according to Samson, that made him stand apart from the crowd after four (4) years of unremitting toil and failure.

By the fifth year in the trading industry, he joined the New York Stock Exchange. The end of that year saw him receive an award, as the most dynamic trader of the Stock Exchange. His turn-over in the trading business experienced exponential growth, to the tune of millions of dollars.

I met Samson at a United Nations Charity function. It was an opportunity to find out first-hand, how he made a success of his business. The answer I got was so intriguing that I decided to title this story from his terse statement he made and I quote, "I attended the University Of Hard Knocks", unquote.

What is pertinent in Samson's case history in the business world corroborates and confirms the principles and precepts espoused earlier in this book, that anyone can Be, Do, or Have whatever he wants in life. All things are possible, so long as these principles become the guiding light in a life-style of discipline and diligence, highlighted in a subsequent summary.

They are as follows:

1. **Who do you listen to?** Apart from listening to those who have what you want, you must be able to enlist the number of authors, gurus, mentors, business colleagues you have listened to and make references to them from time to time.

2. **Willingness to learn and Willingness to accept changes.** What are you willing to invest in order to manifest your dreams? What things will you give up to learn new lessons? Are you willing to change the way you think or feel about things? If you want things in your life to change, you are going to have to change things in your life. Change your thinking without excuses.

3. **Teachability Index.** What is your willingness to learn? Are you Teachable or Coachable? What is your willingness to accept changes of habits? Are you willing to obey your mentors? Can you submit to instructions?

4. **Training Balance Scale.** One side of the Training Balance Scale deals with the mind, associated with thoughts, thinking, desires, goals, attitude, energy, emotions. The other side deals with the physical, associated with actions, movements, steps, plans, activities which is about the "How". You must focus on the "Why" and not the "How".

5. **Unconscious Competence.** You grow from:

   Unconscious incompetence (you don't know that you don't know.)
   Conscious incompetence (you know that you don't know)

Conscious competence (you know that you know)
Unconscious competence (you know that you know automatically)

6. **Master the Basics.** When the foundation is faulty, a house cannot stand. Correct and consistent practice of the fundamental principles is the only way to master the basics.

7. **The Power of Repetition, Affirmation, Study and Discipline.** This is a discipline that compels you to repeat practice of actions and affirmations, including the act of study to strengthen you from within. This is the only way to strengthen your vibration and confidence to create your future.

8. **The Concepts of Energy Frequency.** Everything is vibrating at different frequencies. Your brain is a transmitter and receiver of energy. You have the ability to transmit anything you choose, at a frequency level you choose. By choice you can create your life.

9. **Feel Good Right Now.** It is very important that you feel good no matter what circumstances comes your way. There are three things you need to consider: ONE have a burning desire to achieve something; TWO put strong feelings into your desire; THREE always be in the sweet spot.

10. **The immense Power of Letting Go of the "HOW".** When the student is ready, the teacher will appear. Remain focused on your goal and work diligently with the correct recipes and the "how" will not matter.

11. **Tools and Techniques to raise Your Energy.** When a lot of emotion is attached to your

thoughts, the power and intensity of the thought increases. Listen more to positive messages through audio programs. Read uplifting books and surround yourself with positive and uplifting people. Detoxify and do some cleansing of your body.

12. **Your Beliefs Become your Reality.** When you impose time restraints on when your desires should manifest, you are engaging in lack of thinking and this is counterproductive. Forbid procrastination.

13. **Have a Chief AIM and Depth of Vision.** You must have chief Aim and be obsessed with what you want. This adds power and intensity to your thoughts. You must increase focus and energy towards getting what you want.

14. **How to Plant and Nurture the Seeds to Success.** Setting a goal is like planting a seed. You need to plant it, water it, fertilize it and care for it. Surround yourself with positive vibrations, and you will find circumstances, events, opportunities, and people will begin to appear in your life.

15. **Reading.** Read uplifting books and write down any new discoveries you made from each book to be referred to intermittently in future.

16. **Exploring Societies.** Get to connect and join Societies where you meet with people of like minds to discover more information and opportunities for the taking. You cannot be an island unto yourself.

17. **Health from Rich Nutrient/Plants and Fitness.** There are many discoveries of food nutrition and

supplements to support food intake to enrich your health. Eat fresh organic vegetables and keep fit with regular exercises.

THE ROAD TO SUCCESS IS NOT SMOOTH. SUCCESS ITSELF IS NOT FINAL, FAILURE IS NOT FATAL, IT IS THE WILL TO CONTINUE THAT COUNTS.

CONCLUSIONS

People have lost hope of ever coming out of Poverty or how they can ever acquire Financial Freedom. This book gives the Solution. All that is required is to choose out of the series of suggested Recipe that excites you, and put them through practice of action and passion to the level of "Unconscious Competence". Some of the recipe may sound similar on the surface, but when you "Dig deep" into your regular practice, you discover amazing differences. In the course of time, your vibrational frequency develops a connection to strange situations that shifts favourably towards monetary multiplication. The Core Message of this book is the inculcation of a new life style from the practice of new thinking habits. It is a journey that will expose you to new patterns of positive orientation, from old thought process. You have come to adopt a new process that transforms the vibrational frequency of your Well Being. What you choose from the various options, varies from one person to another, based on expediency or convenience of choice. There is the 99% assurance of success for whoever is willing to attain high teachability index, making use of the adopted doctrines. It works without exception.

Alternatively, there are two short-cut methods recommended as a "daily capsule medication" in the form of a summary, as well as Thunder Affirmations at the end of the book. You can pick either of the ones that excite you the most to confess in less than 15 minutes as a regular ritual. It can be programmed into your daily chores like dosage of drugs, 3 times a day. When this is done consistently on a daily basis and put into "Action" the way you are directed, the same result of accelerated accumulation of wealth becomes your experience.

You are obliged to add to your Daily Capsule the use of this Inspiring Poem. It could take the place of a candle-light to strengthen your spirit, rising above the Storms of Life.

DON'T QUIT!

When things go wrong, as they sometimes will,
When the road you're trudging seems all uphill,
When the funds are low and the debts are high,
And you want to smile, but you have to sigh,
When care is pressing you down a bit,
Rest, if you must, but don't you quit.

Life is queer with its twists and turns,
As every one of us sometimes learns,
And many a failure turns about,
When he might have won had he stuck it out;
Don't give up though the pace seems slow—
You may succeed with another blow.

Often the goal is nearer than,
It seems to a faint and faltering man,
Often the struggler has given up,
When he might have captured the victor's cup,
And he learned too late when the night slipped down,
How close he was to the golden crown.

Success is failure turned inside out—
The silver tint of the clouds of doubt,
And you never can tell how close you are,
It may be near when it seems so far,
So stick to the fight when you're hardest hit-
It's when things seem worst that you must not quit.
—Author unknown

Become a Money Magnet

(Quick Summary)

CONCEPT INTRODUCTION AND PURPOSE: Obedience to the Laws of Money Making and the Seven Principles suggested for accelerated access to wealth.

SUPERNATURAL POWER OF FOCUS: Self-knowers Focus to excel at doing what can be equated to the miraculous because they will always disallow distractions.

THE SUBCONCIOUS MIND: Powerhouse of conviction and energy to build belief and conviction to activate creation.

LAW OF RECIPROCITY: Good gesture begets good return. Connect with people who have what you want to get what you desire. Be teachable.

ANTIDOTE TO EXCUSE DISEASE:

Positively vaccinate yourself against failure on the grounds of health, intelligence, age or luck.

DISCOVER A NEW YOU: Mirror Technique to remind and rehearse presentations without trepidation, using pasted slogans around your room/office to build confidence.

OVERCOMING FEAR: Take a positive action decisively and promptly from positive thoughts and consistently count your blessings before you sleep at night.

AUTOSUGGESTION: Read aloud repeatedly written positive thoughts to feed the "rich garden of your subconscious mind".

PAINT A PICTURE: Paste inspiring pictures and cards around your bedside, wallet and office to inspire your desires, and help them to materialize faster.

LAW OF ATTRACTION: Ask and you shall receive. Allow your Well Being to flow in Harmony with Universal Laws of Vibration, making your desire and belief a vibrational Match. Your request or desire is answered every time you ask without question. Your Well Being is naturally your Legacy and your Source.

COMMAND YOUR WISH: Imagine and plan with confidence a burning desire to make money. The written plan must state the amount, time frame, to be read aloud at least twice a day, backed by enduring faith to succeed. Command your desire for money and it will manifest with time.

HUNTER OF HAPPINESS: Choose thoughts that make you feel good when you think of them. Control how you can feel good in the midst of your experience to progress towards Creation of your happiness.

REMOTE REALITY: Stimulate your imagination by visualizing pleasant situations to delight your mind and activate new vibrations with virtual reality.

DEPTH OF VISION: Rise above trivialities and stretch your imagination. Stimulate your mind by reading books regularly. See beyond how things appear at the moment.

UPGRADE YOUR PROFILE: Act; think that you are important and wealthy. Build a "sell yourself to yourself commercial" to be reminded you are a first-class person.

RESOLUTIONS: Have a mind of your own, but make quick decisions. Develop a listening habit and keep your eyes wide open. Genuine wisdom is noticeably.

DREAM BUILDER: Become a Dream Builder by appealing to your imagination. Always think of new ideas to allow imagination into existence and you are on the road to building a dream.

GREATEST GIFT: Always think positively to radiate happiness and anyone you are holding as your object of attention inherits your vibration.

ACTION HABIT: Be an activationist. Use action to cure fear and gain confidence. Always deal and think in terms of now.

THE NUMBER GAME: A Prosperity Game and powerful tool to fire and expand your desire and vibrational point of attraction towards wealth.

STRONGHOLD OF THE MASTERMIND: Organized power of collected brains working in harmony for wealth creation.

TIME: Killing Time is not "murder", it is "suicide". Time is more than money and so you must programme and have purpose in life every available moment.

CREATIVE: Remove the word "impossible" from your dictionary and cancel out "traditional thinking" from your mindset. Practice listening more than talking to obtain raw materials for creativity.

BELIEF LEVEL: Use Autosuggestion to replace negative dominant thoughts with the positive to raise your faith or belief level.

RAMPAGE OF APPRECIATION: Appreciating pleasant objects and happenings around you in gratitude gives you good feelings, accumulating to Rampage of Appreciation. It is the fastest way to connect with the source of Non-Physical Energy.

UNLIMITIED RESOURCES: There is no lacking but abundance with the universe. Develop Abundance Consciousness.

COOPERATE KNOWLEDGE: A group of special people working in harmony for a common purpose; make everyone in that group knowledgeable and special. Formal education makes a living but self-education makes a fortune.

THE WALLET TECHNIQUE: Powerful tool for boosting your feeling of prosperity and financial point of attraction.

FEELING AFFECTION TOWARDS MONEY: Develop love when paying your bills. Let the spirit of Love guide your attitude towards money in all circumstances.

REMAIN IN ROBUST HEALTH: Your health is your wealth. Your wealth will be a sorrowful experience without good health. Annual Medical check-up is good, but attention should be given to the preventive and miraculous potential of Natural Cures, which has come of age in this generation.

THUNDER AFFIRMATIONS

FOCUS

1. THE SUPERNATURAL POWER OF MY FOCUS FOR EXCELLENCE WILL NEVER SHIFT.

SUBCONSCIOUS MIND

2. MY SUBCONSCIOUS MIND IS LOADED WITH POSITIVE THOUGHTS AND SUCCESS-ASSURANCE, TO VICTORY. I AM SUCCESSFUL IN EVERYTHING I DO.

RECIPROCITY

3. I AM A CARRIER OF GOOD NEWS AND GOOD GESTURE, GENERATING GOOD FORTUNE FROM OBEDIENCE AND BEING TEACHABLE. I RADIATE LOVE AND HAPPINESS EVERY SINGLE DAY.

EXCUSE DISEASE

4. I MAKE NO ROOM FOR COMPLAINS ANYMORE BECAUSE, IT IS BELOW MY BENCHMARK.

OVERCOMING FEAR

5. I FAITHFULLY REPLACE FEAR WITH BLESSINGS BEFORE ANY ACTION. I AM ALWAYS CALM AND RELAXED IN EVERY SITUATION.

LAW OF ATTRACTION

6. I AM LIFTED INTO HIGHER TRUTH TO ATTRACT WHAT I WANT BECAUSE, MY DESIRES AND BELIEFS MATCH WITH THE UNIVERSE. MONEY FLOWS FREELY AND ABUNDANTLY INTO MY LIFE.

COMMAND YOUR WISH

7. I COMMAND WITH ABSOLUTE CONFIDENCE MY DESIRES INTO EXISTENCE EVERY MORNING.

VIRTUAL REALITY

8. I VISUALIZE ONLY PLEASANT SITUATIONS TO DELIGHT MY MIND EVERYDAY. MY HEART IS A MAGNET THAT ATTRACTS MORE OF EVERYTHING I DESIRE.

STEWARDSHIP

9. I RECEIVE BLESSINGS FROM FREE AND FEARLESS STEWARDSHIP TO GIVE, BE GRATEFUL AND GENEROUS.

DEPTH OF VISION

10. I WILL RISE ABOVE TRIVIALITIES TO STRETCH MY IMAGINATION FOR IMPROVEMENT.

UPGRADE YOUR PROFILE

11. I AM ENTITTLED TO A GOLDEN LIFE, BECAUSE MY LIFE IS INTENTIONALLY PROGRAMMED FOR EXCELLENCE (LIFE).

DREAM BUILDER

12. I WILL CREATE A NEW DREAM TO TAKE A POWER OF ITS OWN EVERYDAY. I AM WORTHY OF LOVE TO EASILY MANIFEST MY DREAMS.

GREATEST GIFT

13. I WILL ALWAYS FEEL GOOD IN THE SPIRIT OF VICTORY, BY CONNECTING TO THE SOURCE OF MY WELL-BEING. EVERY CELL OF MY BODY VIBRATES WITH POSITIVE ENERGY.

ACTION HABIT

14. THERE MUST BE PASSION AND ACTION TO EVERYTHING I DO EVERYDAY.

STRONGHOLD OF THE MASTERMIND

15. I MUST ASSOCIATE WITH LIKE-MINDED PEOPLE COLLABORATING TOWARDS POSITIVE PURPOSES.

CREATIVITY

16. THE WORDS "IMPOSSIBLE" AND "TRADITIONAL THINKING" HAVE BEEN REMOVED FROM MY DICTIONARY. MY POTENTIAL IS LIMITLESS.

BELIEF LEVEL

17. I WILL ALWAYS PRONOUNCE POSITVE THOUGHTS TO INFLUENCE MY FIRST STEP OF FAITH.

RAMPAGE OF APPRECIATIION

18. I AM APPRETIATIVE FOR ALL THINGS AROUND ME WITH GRATITUDE, GATHERED TOWARDS ABUNDANCE.

UNLIMITED RESOURCES

19. I MUST DEVELOP OVERFLOWING CONSCIOUSNESS ALL THE TIME. MY LIFE IS FULL OF ABUNDANCE.

CONVICTION

20. FROM THE RIVER OF LIFE THAT NEVER CEASES TO FLOW COMES MY CONVICTION OF VICTORY.

GIVING

21. I MUST GIVE WITH A WILLING HEART, SOMETHING VALUABLE TO SOMEONE EVERYDAY.

HEALTH

22. I MUST LIVE A ROBUST HEALTHY LIFE FROM RICH DIETING, AND REGULAR PHYSICAL EXERCISE EVERYDAY.

GLOSSARY OF WISDOM PROCLAMATIONS

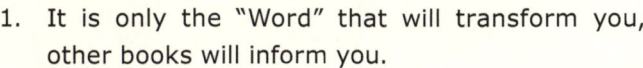

1. It is only the "Word" that will transform you, other books will inform you.
2. Where there is no vision, there will be no direction.
3. Vision unfolds our purpose and our purpose unfolds our destiny.
4. Only disciples will make heaven and not church goers.
5. Worry makes you grow older than your age.
6. Your revelation will determine your manifestation.
7. Those who wait for their turn never miss their time.
8. Your relationship with God (Infinite Intelligence) will determine your consciousness of Him. And your consciousness of Him will determine your security on earth.
9. Your destiny will not change until your dream life changes.
10. God (Infinite Intelligence) does not change until he has executed his promises.
11. No door has the authority to close when the power of sacrifice is speaking upon it.
12. The greater the sacrifice, the greater the power that will be released upon it.

13. Discovery of a problem leads to creation of solution in life.
14. Do not talk about issues, deal with them.
15. It is foolish to win the argument and loose the victory.
16. You are created to add value to creation.

MEDICAL DEFINITIONS

Serotonin is a chemical produced by the body to enable the brain and nervous systems to communicate. Its deficiency can lead to nervous breakdown like depression.

Cortisol is a steroid or stress hormone, known as public enemy number one, that can lead to depression, mental illness or lower your immune function etc.

Endocrine are glands and hormones controlled by stimulation from the nervous system to maintain the body homeostasis.

Homeostasis is the ability of the body or cell to maintain equilibrium or stability within its internal environment, when dealing with external changes.

Fibroblast Growth Factor (FGF) are a family of binding proteins, involved in wound healing, processing proliferation and differentiation of variety of cells, angiogenesis (reformulation of blood vessels), etc.

Neurotransmitters are chemicals that transmit signals throughout our brain and body.

Hormones are chemical messengers travelling through your bloodstream to other organs.

ADOPT A NEW LIFESTYLE

1. Smile Always.
2. Laugh with life in it.
3. Have a Good Posture; look up with your Shoulder up.
4. Cultivate Habit of Book Reading; Listen to Audio/ Video Motivating Talks. Reduce watching daily TV to one hour.
5. Attend Meetings.
6. Daily Meditation and Visitation to Dream Sites and Locations.
7. Create your Dream, using a Dreambook. Check for information, taking pleasant pictures and pasting them to glance at, first thing in the morning and last thing at night.
8. Create a Dream Board with messages like "Debt Free"," Millionaire Money-Magnet", to glance at regularly.
9. Create a Card inscribing boldly your chief AIM in life to be looked at every other time. Visit places to expand your Dreams and Beliefs.
10. HUG People as much as possible. Avoid Gossip.
11. Practice Appreciation, Gratitude and Thankfulness. Make it regular always looking for the good.
12. Look for the Good (GOLD) in People.
13. Speak Positive words and mitigate the Negative.
14. Live Below your Means by Budget.

15. You MUST be Debt-Free.
16. Listen to Pleasant Music.
17. Dress comfortably well and Feel Good for Success.
18. Make New Friends and stay away from Negative People.
19. Say "Please" and "Thank You" Always.
20. Learn and attempt Something New Every day.
21. Do something with your Hands—Draw, Sing, Play Games, Play with a Pet/Child.
22. Organize your Car or Office or Room.
23. Do some Stretching.
24. Get a "Priority Manager Programme" about your Activities.
25. HOPE has two Meanings:
    A. Have Only Positive Expectations.
    B. Help Other People Excel.

26. Always Have A CASH-COW.
27. Connect With Charity Organizations in Your Community.
28. Live, Laugh Love as a way of Life.
29. LIFE means "Live Intentionally for Excellence.
30. Stick to Stay and Get the Pay. Don't quit.

PICK- ONE- AND- WIN
LANDMARK DESTINATIONS

The following website links will transform your life, if you follow the recipes recommended in this book correctly. When you do that, then you have developed a winning attitude to cause a realm of new possibilities, to live an extraordinary life. You will experience improvement in the quality of your personal productivity, wiping out all past negative interpretations of contexts (coded as Rackets), to discover a New You. In the course of this experience, there is a positive permanent shift in your thinking to empower creativity, making you unstoppable.

You need to create multiple streams of income (MSI), to arrive at your ElDorado! Any of these websites will fetch you astonishing income. Every one of them is a winner. All you need to do is to PICK ONE and run with it, while the rest may take second priority along the line. It worked for me to make six-figure income under five months. It will work for you.

www.soltan.myzija.com
www.glitterglowrich.myorganogold.com
www.mylifepharm.com/glowrich
www.karatbars.com/?s=glitterglowrich

Should you require further guidance, which way to go on any of these ventures, simply contact soltansecurity@ hotmail.com or www.accelerateyourabundance.com.

REFERENCES

1. ***ASK AND IT IS GIVEN,*** BY ESTHER & JERRY HICKS. NEW YORK HAY HOUSE 2004.

2. ***THE MAGIC OF BELIEVING,*** BY BRISTOL CLAUDE. NEW YORK POCKET BOOKS 1991.

3. ***THE MAGIC OF THINKING BIG,*** BY DAVID J SCHWARTZ PHD, KANSAS FIRESIDE 1987.

4. ***THINK AND GROW RICH*** BY NAPOLEON HILL, NEW YORK BALLANTINE BOOKS 1987.

5. ***THE SECRET*** BY BYRNE RHONDA. ASTRIA BOOKS 2010.

6. ***THE POWER OF THE SECRET*** BY BYRNE RHONDA, NEW YORK ASTRIA BOOKS 2010.

7. ***YOUR WISH IS YOUR COMMAND*** BY KEVIN TRUDEAU (GLOBAL INFORMATION NETWORK 2011).

8. ***THE LAWS OF WEALTH*** BY JOHNNIE CASS 2010.

9. ***CURES OF OVER 200 DISEASES (ALTERNATIVE RESEARCHED NATURAL CURE),*** BY JOHN AUSTIN.

10. ***SEE YOU AT THE TOP,*** BY ZIG ZIGLER. PELICAN PUBLISHING COMPANY. 2011.

11. ***HOW TO WIN FRIENDS AND INFLUENCE PEOPLE,*** BY DALE CARNEGIE. GALLERY BOOKS 1981.

12. ***LAMININE, A BREAKTHROUGH IN NUTRITION*** BY PETER GLICKMAN.

Edwards Brothers Malloy
Oxnard, CA USA
November 21, 2014